CONTENTS

Front Cover: Julia Virat on the Red Dihedral (5.10), The Incredible Hulk, Sierra Nevada, California. Photo by Calder Davey.
Back Cover: Climbers in Pinnacle Gully, Mt. Washington, NH. Photo by Joe Klementovich.

© 2019 The American Alpine Club

ISBN: 978-0-9998556-5-2; (e-book) 978-0-9998556-7-6. Manufactured in the United States. Published by the American Alpine Club, 710 Tenth Street, Suite 100, Golden, CO, 80401.

WARNING!
The activities described within Accidents in North American Climbing (ANAC)—including but not limited to: rock climbing, ice climbing, mountaineering, backcountry skiing, or any other outdoor activity—carry a significant risk of personal injury or death. The owners, staff, contributors, and volunteers that create this publication recommend that you DO NOT participate in these activities unless you are an expert, have sought or obtained qualified professional instruction or guidance, are knowledgeable about the risks involved, and are willing to assume personal responsibility for all the risks associated with these activities. ANAC and its publisher, the American Alpine Club, MAKE NO WARRANTIES, EXPRESSED OR IMPLIED, OF ANY KIND REGARDING THE CONTENTS OF THIS PUBLICATION, AND EXPRESSLY DISCLAIM ANY WARRANTY REGARDING THE ACCURACY OR RELIABILITY OF INFORMATION CONTAINED HEREIN. The American Alpine Club further disclaims any responsibility for injuries or death incurred by any person engaging in these activities. Use the information contained in this publication at your own risk, and do not depend on the information contained herein for personal safety or for determining whether to attempt any climb, route, or activity described herein. The examples/stories contained herein are anecdotal and/or informational only and are not intended to represent advice, recommendations, or commentary on appropriate conduct, standards or choices that you, the reader, may make regarding your own activities.

ACCIDENTS IN NORTH AMERICAN CLIMBING

Volume 11 | Number 4 | Issue 72

American Alpine Club

EDITOR EMERITUS
John E. (Jed) Williamson

EDITOR
Dougald MacDonald

SENIOR EDITOR
R. Bryan Simon

CONTRIBUTING EDITORS
Aram Attarian, Dave Weber

REGIONAL EDITORS
Daniel Apodaca (Southwest); Aram Attarian
(Southeast); Lindsay Auble (KY); Mark Berenblum
(Upstate NY); Dan Cousins (New England); Stacia
Glenn (WA); Sarah Koniewicz (Midwest); Bret
Rhinesmith (WY); R. Bryan Simon (WV); Eric
Ratkowski (Shawangunks, NY); Lee Smith (CO);
Dave Weber (AK); Michael Wejchert (NH)

DESIGN
David Boersma – Mojave Creative Lab

ADDITIONAL THANKS
Frank Carus, Dan Cousins, Derek DeBruin, Ron
Funderburke, Leo Paik, Jim Pasterczyk, Mike
Riley, Azissa Singh

Alpine Club of Canada

CANADA EDITOR
Robert Chisnall
anam@alpineclubofcanada.ca

MOJAVE
CREATIVE LAB

WE BELIEVE IN
▌PREPARATION

Every expedition starts with a plan. Our success in the wild depends on experience and thoughtful packing for the trail ahead. At Mojave Creative Lab, we help your brand prepare for the summit.

GRAPHIC DESIGN
for the trail ahead.

mojavecreativelab.com

PREFACE

By Dougald MacDonald

I went sport climbing yesterday at a crag near my home, and at the top of each route was a pair of "mussy hooks" attached to the anchor. Generous climbers had recently replaced the chains on these 20-year-old routes with big steel hooks with snap-link-style gates. After leading each pitch, we hung quickdraws from the anchor bolts for top-roping, and then, when it came time to clean the pitch, the last climber just dropped the rope into the hooks, cleaned the draws, and lowered off.

Drop-in anchor hooks (sometimes called mussy hooks) are showing up at more and more crags, and, in my opinion, this is a great development. Anchor hooks eliminate fatal mistakes when untying, threading the rope through an anchor, and retying. They greatly reduce the chance of communication errors, where the belayer on the ground and the climber at the anchor are out of sync—lowering becomes the de facto choice. Moreover, this is the anchor that many new leaders learn to use first, when they reach the top of their first gym climbs.

Now, *of course*, every climber still needs to learn how to tie through traditional anchors and to rappel safely. These are essential skills for outdoor climbing. And anchor hooks come with their own issues. For example, it's unsafe to climb above hooks without clipping the rope to the anchor separately with quickdraws. Hooks need to be replaced periodically (as do all anchors). It's preferable to clip your own quickdraws for top-roping, either as the primary anchor or as backups for hooks. Nevertheless, there is growing consensus that the pros of anchor hooks significantly outweigh the cons. Looking over the last few editions of ANAC, at least half a dozen fatalities and many serious injuries might have been avoided if climbers had found these hooks at the top of single-pitch routes instead of traditional anchors with chains.

Most areas have enthusiastic locals who install or maintain anchor hardware. Seek them out and encourage them to start using climbing-specific anchor hooks. Better yet, give them 25 or 50 bucks to buy some. Donate to your local climbing organization and suggest they organize a re-anchoring day. Support the American Safe Climbing Association, which purchases hooks for climbers to install. Anchor hooks aren't appropriate or practical everywhere, but on thousands of climbs with existing bolted anchors, installing hooks will create a safer and more enjoyable experience.

Submissions

Share your story and help fellow climbers! Visit *publications.americanalpineclub.org* to file an accident report online. Or email us at *accidents@americanalpineclub.org*.

Friends of Accidents in North American Climbing

The following people recently have donated $100 or more specifically to support *Accidents in North American Climbing*. Thank you! Make your own contribution at *americanalpineclub.org/donate*.

Stuart & Marcella Bernstein
Christian Cannon
Laura Chedalawada
Carla Firey

Eric Green
Mike McWherter
Scott Petersen
Eric Pyne

John & Rebecca Soebbing
Timothy Wilt

THE SHARP END

Join the nearly 40,000 people who listen to the Sharp End podcast each month. Hosted by Ashley Saupe, the Sharp End features interviews with climbers, rangers, and rescue professionals, based on the stories in *Accidents in North American Climbing*.

The Sharp End is sponsored for 2019 by Mammut, with additional support from Colorado Outward Bound School, Suunto, and other companies. Find it wherever you listen to podcasts.

AAC RESCUE BENEFITS

Membership in the American Alpine Club qualifies you for rescue benefits in case things go wrong during human-powered activities beyond the trailhead (except for those at sea). With up to $12,500 available, we've got you covered.

Trailhead Rescue
- $7,500 in global coverage, including the United States
- No elevation restriction
- Member discount on expanded coverage
- 37 AAC members were rescued or received assistance in 2018
- To use the Trailhead Rescue Benefit, members must call Global Rescue at (617) 459-4200 as soon as possible during an emergency

Domestic Rescue Benefit
- Up to $5,000 in reimbursement for out-of-pocket rescue expenses within the U.S. only. Canada and Mexico are excluded.
- File a claim within 60 days of rescue by emailing claims@americanalpineclub.org or by calling (303) 384-0110
- Medical and ambulance expenses do not qualify
- Reimbursement subject to verification and approval

Activities Covered
Climbing, hiking, backcountry skiing, mountain biking, and more. If it's human-powered and not on the sea, and you're rescued, you're covered as long as you're an active AAC member. Note: Basic coverage does not include search, ambulance services, or medical care.

Upgrades
Planning to climb internationally? We recommend upgrading to a full Global Rescue membership with a 5 percent AAC discount. Upgrades include field rescue, medical consultation, and evacuation. Learn more at americanalpineclub.org/rescue or call 1-800-381-9571.

Slippery stone, rockfall, diving birds—these hazards all exist independent of any human activity. They only become "risks" when climbers confront them. Here, Nick Schlichtman accepts the challenge on Inner Space (5.11b R) in Eldorado Canyon, Colorado. *Rob Kepley*

Know the Ropes

MANAGING RISK

Planning and Reflection for Rock Climbers

BY RON FUNDERBURKE & DEREK DEBRUIN

Last year millions of viewers were awed by *Free Solo*, the feature film that documented Alex Honnold's historic solo ascent of El Capitan. We were stupefied by the level of free climbing ability and mental strength required to even conceive of this feat, much less achieve it. We also were captivated by the debate that ensued. Many commentators viewed Alex's climb as a moral failing, and many harangued the system that would allow such an ascent and the society that would laud it.

The debate begs some questions: How do we perceive risk as rock climbers? How do we manage it? Do we consistently manage risk? What are the most common inconsistencies? Even if we all have different relationships to risk, isn't the desire to challenge ourselves in a complex and dangerous environment at least part of our essential motivation to climb? Is it possible that we all have more in common with Alex Honnold than we think?

In this article, we'll take a closer look at the real risks in rock climbing. We'll point out our most common strategies for managing those risks. We'll point to some of the most common inconsistencies in those strategies—moments where our human weaknesses are revealed. Finally, we'll propose strategies for analysis and self-reflection. If we are striving to have a clear-eyed conversation about risk, we can learn something from every single climb, regardless of the outcome.

THE RISK CYCLE

In this conversation about risk, words and presumed meanings of words matter. Dictionaries suggest the words "hazard" and "risk" are synonymous, but the scholarship surrounding this subject describes a much different relationship between these words. We're going to describe risk as a cycle, wherein hazards exist objectively, our exposure to those hazards subjectively creates an opportunity for loss as well as reward, and the outcome of our exposure can be analyzed.

HAZARDS

Hazards exist objectively—they are dangerous regardless of whether humans are ever exposed to them. They can be listed, and they can be anticipated. But they are not absolute values. To understand them, we must understand the interrelationship between the probability of an occurrence and the consequence. For example, we know that humans cannot breathe underwater and therefore prolonged submersion is likely to kill a person. There is an extreme potential consequence. But we tend to assess a low probability of that consequence when competent adults go swimming. We also can nullify the probability of drowning simply by staying out of the water.

Most assessments of hazards can be divided into four distinct groups. Here are some examples of how each group applies in climbing:

High-Probability/Low-Consequence	High-Probability/High-Consequence
• Falling in challenging fifth-class terrain with mitigation techniques (belay, protection, etc.) in place • Falls while bouldering with spotters and pads	• Afternoon thunderstorm with lightning • Ground fall before first piece of protection • Fall while free soloing at your limit
Low-Probability/Low-Consequence	Low-Probability/High-Consequence
• Dropping equipment • Major gobies from hand jams • Tripping on the trail to the crag • Tweaked finger	• Lowering or rappelling off the end of the rope • Catastrophic rockfall • Severed rope • Easy free soloing

When the probability and the consequence of a hazard are low, we tend to accept those risks routinely—think of exposure to a poisonous plant or a non-venomous snakebite. When the probability and the consequence of a hazard are high, we tend to avoid these hazards—think of lightning storms or avalanches.

In the nebulous regions between those extremes, most climbers are willing to expose themselves to hazards because there are mitigation techniques to diminish either the consequence or the likelihood of a negative outcome—and because the perceived value of the risk-taking (that is, going climbing) is high.

For example, a high-probability/low-consequence situation would be an average climbing fall, whether leading, top-roping, or bouldering. As long as the key mitigation techniques are in place (effective equipment and competent climbers), it is unlikely the consequences will be too severe. Similarly, many climbing approaches involve brief exposure to drop-offs or catwalks. We perceive a low probability of a bad outcome on features like these, even though we see that a fall would be deadly. And, instead of just accepting such hazards, we can mitigate them through rope-team travel, quick belays, or spotting.

RISK

Risk happens when climbers expose themselves to hazards, which introduces a variety of human factors into the risk cycle. This can alter predicted probabilities, create consequences where none previously existed, and negate mitigation tactics. To accurately understand risk, we need to understand how prone to error we can be.

For example, we all know what it feels like to climb challenging fifth-class terrain. If the route is very difficult for us, falls are likely. If all of our mitigation techniques are effective (the equipment, the anchor and protection, the belay) we can confidently accept those risks. But humans are fallible. We forget a key step; we overlook important details; we miscommunicate. If a single human factor has compromised a climber's mitigation techniques, the most benign top-rope outing can shift into a high-consequence event.

On the other side of the spectrum, a similar miscalculation happens when our dread of severe and deadly outcomes causes us to *overestimate* the likelihood of a high-consequence event. When we overmanage one risk, we often open the door for another hazard. For example, climbing teams who indulge extra time and deliberation in the construction of their belay anchors may inadvertently expose themselves to afternoon thunderstorms and lightning.

BIASES

Behavioral psychology tells us that humans are subject to a panoply of cognitive biases. We make choices that we perceive to be rational yet may be rife with error or inaccurate perception. Particularly in climbing, dubious practices and specious techniques can have fatal outcomes. Consequently, climbers should pay attention to three particular cognitive biases: confirmation, optimism, and commitment.

Confirmation bias is the tendency to interpret new information as confirmation of existing belief. The confidence required to successfully lead a pitch often means that climbers harbor positive self-assessments—we think of ourselves as being good at climbing, and further, we presume that when things go well the outcome is due to the actions we took. It becomes easy for a confident climber to think they've done everything right when nothing bad happened, even if, in fact, they were simply lucky in a low-probability/high-consequence environment.

Optimism bias causes us to believe that negative outcomes are less likely to happen to us specifically, or that positive outcomes are more likely for us. We might think, "Of course I will make it off the summit before the afternoon storm." "I won't pitch off this easy but run-out climbing." "I would never miss the pads when I fall." Each time optimism bias surfaces these thoughts, confirmation bias is reinforced.

Commitment bias describes one's commitment to a goal or outcome—the "summit or die" mentality. Unfortunately, such strong commitment to a goal can often lead to a "summit *and* die" outcome.

Each of these biases can be alleviated to some extent with candid reflection on the outcomes of every climb, especially with an honest and objective partner.

OUTCOME

After exposure to any risk, many climbers have a binary perception of the outcome. The climb was a success or the climb was a failure. If the climb was successful, many climbers will attribute every aspect of the day to that success. If the climb was unsuccessful, every moment of the day will be construed as a failure. These attributions are common cognitive errors.

A binary conception of a climb's outcome can have terribly unproductive results. Climbers willingly overlook many aspects of their day that might offer substantial experiential insight. If the climb is successful, hardships and near misses are often characterized as an unavoidable part of the sport—Type 2 fun. It's only when accidents occur, or we experience a really eye-opening close call, that we dig into the aspects of the day that could paint a portrait of causation. Sadly, even on those days, many climbers are unwilling to self-assess for the fallibilities and complacency that might produce tragic outcomes.

Sam Latone celebrates a difficult new route in Utah. At such moments, it's wise to ask: Was this an unqualified success? What could we learn from it? *Derek DeBruin*

Instead of rushing to our rewards or diving into our despair after a climb, we might consider every outcome a rich learning opportunity. Risk-oriented reflection helps a climber and partner(s) ask a crucial question: "If we did that climb again, what would we do differently?" If we live under the illusion that our successes are entirely based on our skill and excellence, while our failures are entirely based on bad luck, we will never develop an accurate assessment of our powers as risk managers.

ACTIONS FOR EVERY OUTING

Understanding the risk cycle and considering what we're really up against, how can we improve our practice as climbers? How do we grapple with the biases in our judgment and decision-making? What systems will give us a backup when self-awareness wanes?

If your climbing practices and conversations with partners already have a certain cadence and routine, trying some of the things described below can seem awkward at first. For example, if you're already doing some preclimb research and planning (weather forecasts, descent descriptions, emergency preparedness), even more preparation might seem like overthinking the climb. However, in incremental steps, incorporating these suggestions into every outing can help you counter the human factors and cognitive biases that accompany the best-laid plans.

HAZARD INVENTORY FOR BASTILLE CRACK (5 PITCHES, 5.8), ELDORADO CANYON, COLORADO	
High-Probability/Low-Consequence	**High-Probability/High-Consequence**
Well-protected falls Dropped gear from overhead Crowds of climbers	Unprotected falls Afternoon lightning
Mitigation plan: Early start, body-length protection frequency, plenty of gear on rack, attentive belaying, helmets, assisted-braking devices for leader	Carefully and deliberately avoid these risks
Low-Probability/Low-Consequence	**Low-Probability/High-Consequence**
Unfortunately timed need to poop Unleashed chihuahua at the base	Natural rockfall, falling on 4th-class descent, severed rope
Accept these risks	Mitigation plan: Early start, helmets, travel as rope team through exposed section, manage rope line to avoid sharp edges

BEFORE THE CLIMB

Hazard Inventory. A hazard inventory can accompany a careful analysis of a weather forecast, the topo, and other beta. It could be little more than a five-minute conversation with your partner. Try to envision the hazards and make some anticipatory decisions about which risks the team will accept, which ones they will avoid, which risks will require mitigation to reduce the likelihood or probability of a negative outcome, and which human factors are most likely to complicate the overall risk. This kind of conversation also can help new climbing partners get on the same page about their acceptable level of risk.

Pre-Mortem. In this brainstorming exercise, the party takes some time before a climb to imagine various outcomes and speculate on how they might come to pass. It's valuable

	PRE-MORTEM BRAINSTORM: BASTILLE CRACK, ELDORADO CANYON			
Outcomes	Outcome 1: We climb efficiently to the top without incident.	Outcome 2: We climb to the top, but we're delayed by one or more incidents.	Outcome 3: We don't make it to the top. We have to bail.	Outcome 4: We're involved in an accident.
What events led to this outcome?	We managed our rope well. We climbed smoothly. We placed solid protection and built anchors appropriately. We had no trouble with route-finding. We had great weather, and there were no unanticipated delays.	There was a party in front of us. We had a hard time hearing each other. I took a fall, and I needed tension from the belayer several times. The descent was confusing. We struggled with a tangled rope.	We climbed a weird off-route variation. Our delays accumulated, and it began to get dark. We lost our psych. We were worried about the descent.	I took a risk on a big move, and I didn't make it. I fell farther than expected and broke my ankle.

Chart continues on next page...

What would we have done differently?	Put cold beverages in a cooler to enjoy while we debrief the climb.	Practice rope management in a ground-school setting. Do more single-pitch cragging at the same grade. Start earlier to avoid other parties.	Find more beta before the next climb. Pack headlamps. Build up to a five-pitch climb with more two- or three-pitch routes.	Place more gear to protect difficult moves and eliminate runouts. Pull on gear if necessary to avoid consequential falls.
What will we do when we encounter this outcome?	We'll be sure to debrief, not missing an opportunity to learn from the climb, even if it's just to review what we did well.	We'll be patient. We'll try to learn. We'll bring enough supplies to be comfortable during delays and plan our day so a delay is OK.	We'll make an honest self assessment when delays begin. Bring enough equipment to bail stress-free. Find satisfaction in having bailed safely.	Call for help. Be ready to package ankle. Tandem rappel and/or lower to the ground. Come back to retrieve gear with another partner.

because it asks the party to anticipate a non-binary perception of how the day might go. For each imagined outcome, the party should ask some important questions.

Self Assessment. For climbers, self assessment is challenging. One's individual desire to do a climb, the pressures of ego and performance, and the obligation we feel to our partners all influence self assessment. These external pressures make it difficult to recognize when you are not at your best and when your performance—even if it may be successful—will not be optimal. Asking yourself some important questions before an outing, before a crux, before any risk, helps disrupt the external blinders. In some cases, the answers will keep a climber from getting into situations they should not have accepted without being 100 percent prepared and committed.

SELF ASSESSMENT QUESTIONNAIRE	
Do I want to do this climb today?	Are conditions good?
Have I had enough sleep?	Am I distracted by personal concerns?
Am I healthy?	Have we made a solid plan?
Am I fit?	Am I communicating well with my partner?
Am I feeling rushed?	Am I motivated by something deep and personal?
Is my partner equally or more competent?	What external pressures could be affecting my self assessment?

DURING THE CLIMB

Poise and Attention Self assessment should continue throughout a climb, guiding one's readiness for a crux move, a difficult clip, or an unroped scramble on the descent. When such fateful moments arise, distraction is a dangerous bedfellow. It's time for conversations to cease, for cell phones to be silenced, for the surrounding din to be muted or ignored. Focus is crucial.

Photo: Ron Funderburke

CRITICAL TIMES TO FOCUS

- Tying in
- Setting up the belay
- Rigging a rappel
- High-consequence moves
- Topping out a boulder
- Unroped downclimbing or scrambling

Backups on Lowers, Belays, and Rappels. Backups are one of the most common ways to disrupt human factors that arise from haste, fatigue, and fluster. Once practiced to proficiency, they are so quick to apply that it's difficult to imagine ever going without them.

Closing the System. Managing both ends of the rope is one of the most common preventive practices, because it's a clean and efficient way to account for human factors. Very experienced and thoughtful climbers have been lowered off or rappelled off the end of a rope because some insidious human factor crept into their climbing routine. An unfamiliar rope, an unfamiliar crag, or an inattentive belayer can upset a career's worth of uneventful lowers and rappels.

Redundancy is an idea and a practice that manages the same kinds of human factors as backups. For example, anchors rely on bolts or other protection placed by fallible people in rock evaluated by fallible people. Therefore, we rely on multiple strands of anchor-building material, multiple placements, and multiple rock features to achieve a system with a built-in margin of error.

Systems for Communication and for Frequent Tasks. Clear, rote communication is the closest most climbers will come to a checklist or flowchart—the tools used in many risky fields (medicine, aviation, search and rescue) to avoid mishap. Systematized processes such as universal belay commands disrupt a slew of human factors. No climber intentionally leaves locking carabiners unlocked in critical applications—and yet this step is forgotten. No climber intentionally leans into the abyss without being anchored—and yet experienced climbers fall to their deaths every year. Establishing personalized systems for frequent tasks helps create efficiency and reduce error, whether it's for pre-climb doublechecks, cleaning an anchor, or changing leads on a multipitch route. Such systems should be reviewed regularly and updated when new information or techniques are available.

Helmets and Assisted-Braking Devices. Since rockfall, whether natural or climber trig-gered, is such a common occurrence at many climbing venues, a helmet is one of the logical mitigation techniques climbers deploy. The choice *not* to wear a helmet is also common in situations where rockfall is perceived to be unlikely, such as bouldering or at the climbing gym. Similarly, assisted-braking devices (ABD) give lead climbers a backup if anything unexpected were to compromise the belayer, like overhead rockfall, fatigue, distraction, or a medical emergency.

REFLECTION AND ONGOING LEARNING

Specific mitigation tools and techniques can be learned in a variety of ways and safely practiced to mastery. However, underlying each of them is the greater tool of reflection. When we reflect on our climbing, scrutinizing every action and decision, we learn things that otherwise might elude our awareness and consideration.

What specifically can we do to aid our reflective process? We can begin with the assumption that we do not know everything and that even our best performance can be improved. We can strive for an intentional rationale for each decision we make on a climb. We can stop always doing things simply because we were taught a certain way, but instead make choices that serve to minimize our risk and maximize our chance of success. Allowing for continual growth is how we walk the long path toward mastery—and ultimately what keeps climbing interesting.

After a climb, a party might discuss the effectiveness of their planning—notably, was there a plan in the first place? (A plan might be complex as the logistics for a Grade VI wall or as simple as confirming a climber will lower from the top of a sport climb.) How did the climb actually unfold, and how did this differ from the plan?

Asking yourself "why" at the end of an outing may be the most important tool for mitigating risk. Why did we choose to start at 10 a.m. instead of 6 a.m.? Why did we bring a double rack instead of a single? Next, when was the party most at risk? Were hazards identified? Was exposure to these hazards minimized? Was vulnerability reduced?

It's wise to mix up the process for these reflections. After big objectives, the process might be somewhat formal. Maybe the climbing team will debrief by working through each question together and recording their answers. Conversely, after an afternoon of cragging or a trip to the gym, the questions might be more personal and internal—just a few minutes of thought and inquiry.

Keep in mind that frequent consideration of plans, hazards, and inefficiency can breed its own form of complacency—a sense of control in an inherently uncontrollable environment. This can be combatted by acknowledging what was beyond your power to control. The weather, the rock quality, other climbers, and many other factors cannot be controlled by any single person, yet each can have very real impacts on a climb.

Finally, the party might consider what went well. Even when climbers fail to reach their desired high point, they surely did some things correctly. And when a climb has been wildly successful, it's certainly acceptable to acknowledge the factors that might have led to such a positive outcome. These are the things to remember and emulate on subsequent outings.

From here the process simply begins again with the next climb: Review the prior lessons learned, make a new plan, execute, reflect, repeat.

Ron Funderburke is the education director of the AAC. Derek DeBruin is a climbing guide and outdoor educator based in Utah's northern Wasatch.

Mt. Washington from the east, with Tuckerman Ravine on the far left and Huntington Ravine at far right. The rime-covered observatory buildings can be seen on top. *Brian Post*

Danger Zones
MT. WASHINGTON

By Dougald MacDonald

At just 6,288 feet above sea level, Mt. Washington, the high point of the northeastern United States, packs a very serious mountain into a diminutive package. Home of the so-called "worst weather in the world," Mt. Washington clocked a wind speed of 231 mph in 1934, and hurricane-force gusts (greater than 74 mph) are observed at the summit more than 100 days a year, on average. The summit observatory has recorded temperatures as low as -50°F (-46°C), and an estimated wind chill of -102°F was recorded in January 2004.

Rising at the intersection of major storm tracks and forming a prominent barrier to winds from the west, Mt. Washington and the Presidential Range also receive heavy precipitation. Each season averages 280 inches of snow, and wind-blown snow can pile up to depths of 10 to 40 feet in the east-facing ravines. Yet warmer temperatures can also be a problem, as freezing rain and fog—prime hypothermia conditions—are frequently encountered.

Despite the weather, Mt. Washington draws thousands of adventurers every year for hiking, ski mountaineering, and ice climbing. The access is easy—just 2.5 miles of hiking or skinning from the Joe Dodge Lodge at Pinkham Notch bring you to tree line—and naturally some people get into trouble. According to the Mount Washington Avalanche Center, every year an average of 25 people require rescue assistance on the mountain. Nearly 150 people have died.

This article examines where and why climbing and skiing accidents occur on Mt. Washington and suggests a few steps to prevent them. Although some of these situations are unique to the Presidential Range, many of the lessons apply to mountains throughout North America.

Our focus is on technical climbing (mostly in winter) and skiing, primarily in the dramatic bowls and chutes on the east side of the mountain. Ski activity peaks in the spring season and is centered on Tuckerman Ravine, known as the "birthplace of extreme skiing" in North America. Ice climbing is mostly in Huntington Ravine, to the north of Tuckerman, where multi-pitch gullies draw hundreds each winter.

We looked into the archives of both the Mount Washington Avalanche Center (MWAC) and *Accidents in North American Climbing* (ANAC). We reviewed 152 MWAC reports, from June 2019 back to the beginning of 1998. We also looked at 38 reports published in ANAC between 1978 and 2018. No accidents were duplicated in the various statistics presented in this article. However, each person injured or involved in a given accident was counted, so one report could generate multiple "incidents."

For this article, we only considered incidents that occurred at or above tree line, which is approximately 4,400 feet above sea level, just above the base of the great bowls on the east face. Some hiking also was examined. Normally, ANAC does not cover hiking incidents, but on Mt. Washington in the winter months, nearly all travel above tree line can be considered winter mountaineering.

WHEN AND WHERE

This is very much a story of the winter and spring seasons. Nearly 95 percent of the incidents we tracked occurred from January to May, with more than half of the total in March and April. With one or two exceptions, rock climbs on Mt. Washington are not popular, and there are relatively few climbing accidents in the summer and autumn months. (Hiking incidents occur throughout the year.)

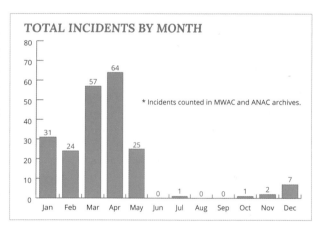

Skiing and avalanche incidents peak in April, when the classic spring sliding in Tuckerman Ravine and the neighboring chutes draws hordes of people to brave the steep slopes and sunbathe and cheer from the floor of the ravine.

In and near Tuckerman Ravine, the three most frequent incident locations are the Lion Head winter trail, the primary summit route in winter conditions; Hillman's Highway, a long chute left (south) of Tuckerman, very popular among skiers; and the Headwall/Lip area of the main bowl. The ski routes in Chute and the Right Gully also see many accidents.

In Huntington Ravine, Central Gully (an easy ice climb or snow climb—or a ski route in certain conditions) and Odell's Gully (WI2/3) have seen the most accidents. The third most frequent location is below the climbs, on the snowy approach, especially on the Fan, the snow-covered boulderfield that spreads below the main gullies.

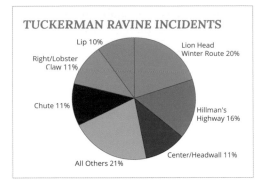

TUCKERMAN RAVINE INCIDENTS

- Lip 10%
- Lion Head Winter Route 20%
- Right/Lobster Claw 11%
- Chute 11%
- Hillman's Highway 16%
- Center/Headwall 11%
- All Others 21%

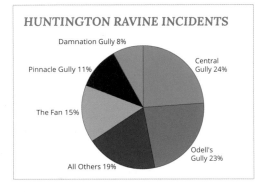

HUNTINGTON RAVINE INCIDENTS

- Damnation Gully 8%
- Central Gully 24%
- Pinnacle Gully 11%
- The Fan 15%
- Odell's Gully 23%
- All Others 19%

FALLS ON SNOW AND ICE

As with most climbing areas, the most common accidents on Mt. Washington are falls—in this case falls on snow or ice. In Tuckerman Ravine, skier falls outnumber climbing and winter mountaineering falls. In Huntington, ice climbing accidents make up the majority, but falls on snow also are significant, especially on the Fan.

A significant factor all over Mt. Washington is the presence of very hard or icy snow resulting from rain/freeze or thaw/freeze events. In such conditions, there may be widespread expanses of snow as hard and slippery as ice, and climbers or skiers who are not prepared with the necessary skills and equipment may suffer long sliding falls. Boulders and bushes below popular routes add to the hazard. The Lion Head winter mountaineering route has seen many accidents when hikers or climbers with inadequate winter boots or no crampons have fallen and slid into trees.

In many reported cases, people involved in falls were either not prepared for hard snow (e.g., they did not carry crampons or ice axes) or they left the necessary gear in the pack. Pull out your ice axe and put on crampons *before* entering steep, icy terrain. Other falls were the result of a failure to self-arrest or loss of control of a glissade. In March 2016, after a thaw/freeze event, a mountaineer glissading on the summit cone lost control and suffered a broken femur. Several skiing accidents have resulted from the failure to stop slides using self-arrest pole grips, such as Whippets. Self-arrest is not an intuitive skill—it must be learned and practiced regularly—and the climber or skier also must recognize the conditions in which it will not be effective. On icy 35° to 45° slopes, self-arrest is unlikely to succeed—it's most important to avoid falling in the first place.

The time of day also plays a key role. As one MWAC accident analysis put it, "Spring skiing is all about timing. Start your day too early and the snow will still be frozen; end your day too late and your slope might turn to cement as you watch. A knowledgeable Tuckerman spring skier will follow the sun, often starting the day on east- or northeast-facing slopes, and slowly work their way across the bowl, ending the day on south-facing slopes that are catching the last of the sun's rays.... Once a [sunny] slope goes into the shade, it can freeze almost instantly, necessitating the use of crampons on the way up and creating no-fall territory on the way down."

Occasionally, falls happen when ice climbers delay roping up during their approach. In February 2016, for example, an inexperienced climber fell from low in

Central Gully as the leader of the party coached the unroped climber up a short ice step below their planned rope-up spot. Note: If you *do* rope up, belays or running protection are essential; otherwise, a fall risks pulling off the entire party.

A somewhat surprising hazard, given that there are no glaciers in New England, is the formation of crevasses in the deep snowpack. Tuckerman Ravine develops bands of crevasses on and below the Headwall. In early April 2012, a man suffered a fatal accident when he slipped while descending into Tuckerman and slid into a crevasse; this party had ascended a different route and thus was unaware of the waiting crevasse hazard.

ICE CLIMBING FALLS

The weather and elevation on Mt. Washington allow for a long ice season, from mid-autumn well into spring. Although most of the climbs are not technically very difficult (up to WI3+), they are complicated by length and exposure to wind, cold, and extremely variable conditions. Climbers can expect ice to shatter and "dinner plate" in cold conditions. Conversely, ice dams may form in bulges, releasing sudden flows of water from tool placements. In 2001, Ned Green, caretaker of the Harvard Mountaineering Club cabin below Huntington Ravine, fell to his death after his soloing partner's tool ruptured an ice dam above him in Damnation Gully.

Pinnacle Gully in Huntington Ravine is the most coveted climb on the mountain. *Joe Klementovich*

Often, poor surface ice must be chopped away to find good tool and screw placements, and longer ice screws may be desirable for protection. In February 1986, a leader fall on brittle and poorly bonded ice in Pinnacle Gully ripped out the ice protection at the belay anchor and resulted in both climbers falling to the bottom of the route and then another 500 feet down the rock-studded Fan below.

A significant hazard on some climbs is the formation of wind slab in surface snow, and a number of ice climbing falls have been associated with small slides that pushed climbers off or caused them to lose their balance. In early March 2013, a climber fell to his death from the second pitch of Pinnacle Gully when he triggered a wind slab about 20 feet wide. Two similar incidents in Odell's Gully have resulted in fatalities Carefully assess the avalanche conditions on your particular route, on the day of the climb, before proceeding.

Placing an extra screw or two can help minimize the seriousness of some falls. In late December 1998, two experienced ice climbers were simul-climbing up Odell's Gully when one snagged a crampon point on his clothing and fell, pulling the other off. The single screw between the two held them both, but one climber fell nearly 40 meters and was injured.

AVALANCHES

April is the peak month for reported avalanche incidents, despite a more stable spring snowpack—this is likely because more people are in Tuckerman Ravine that month. Winter-like storms can deposit significant fresh snow and form dangerous conditions throughout the ski season (i.e., well into May). The archives show that January was the second-highest month for avalanche incidents. Midwinter skiing activity in the ravines has increased significantly in recent years.

A majority of avalanches involve skiers, but climbers and hikers also get caught, especially in the area where winter routes pass near the top of Tuckerman Ravine and in locations all over Huntington Ravine. Most of the reported avalanches were triggered by people, not naturally occurring.

A complicating factor on Mt. Washington, especially in the spring, is large crowds of skiers. This can cause multiple parties to be in the path of any avalanche that is triggered. The crowds and party atmosphere also may encourage poor decision-making and heuristic traps, including the "social proof" trap ("All those guys skied it, so it's got to be OK.")

The recommended avalanche and weather forecast for climbers and skiers is posted at *mountwashingtonavalanchecenter.org* throughout the winter and spring seasons; detailed weather forecasts for the summit are posted at *mountwashington. org*. Winter travelers should read forecasts carefully and then make informed decisions without following others into trouble.

Note that in our examination of the MWAC archives, more avalanche incidents occurred when conditions were rated "Moderate" than when they were rated "Considerable" or "High." A rating of "Moderate" indicates "heightened avalanche conditions on specific terrain features." Given the complexity and steepness of Mt. Washington's terrain, skiers and climbers must evaluate each slope or gully individually.

Another concern is that many climbers and even many skiers do not carry beacons or avalanche rescue gear, and many also do not have adequate avalanche training. In January 2016, a slide in the Chute caught five climbers and skiers, none of whom were wearing beacons or carrying probes and shovels. As the MWAC report for this incident said, "Avalanche gear may or may not save your life should you get caught, but it certainly won't help you if it is in your closet."

WEATHER AND NAVIGATION

Given the extreme weather on Mt. Washington, the number of hypothermia and frostbite cases in the archives is surprisingly low, although storms, whiteout, and disorientation have led to a number of high-profile fatalities or loss of limbs from frostbite. It's also likely that some frostbite cases are not reported, and that storms often result in "near misses" that easily might have become much more serious.

Anyone venturing above tree line on Mt. Washington—especially those planning to travel above the ravines on the Alpine Garden or summit cone—should prepare for extreme wind chill with windproof gloves or mittens (and extras in the pack), a face mask or balaclava, and goggles, in addition to the usual winter clothing. The equipment (GPS and/or map and compass) and skill for navigating in a complete whiteout are also necessities. A frequent challenge arises when layers covering the face lead to foggy goggles freezing over, rendering them useless; consider carrying spares.

Climbers exiting the ice routes in Huntington Ravine are vulnerable to sudden exposure to foul weather. Study the descent options before a climb, especially the Escape Hatch route, which allows a quick descent from the south rim. (Be aware that ice and avalanche hazard may exist in this gully.) Though not as easy, scrambling down from routes on the north side of Huntington may be much safer than attempting to traverse the Alpine Garden to the south. The ability to construct V-thread rappel anchors will allow you to bail directly down certain routes.

The higher you go on Mt. Washington, the worse conditions get. Gear up early. *Joe Klementovich*

EXPECT ANYTHING

Many incidents on Mt. Washington involve a combination or accumulation of factors: a sudden whiteout leading to stranding and frostbite; a slow climb resulting in a descent in darkness, which ends in avalanche terrain. In one tragic example from February 1979, two young ice climbers finished Odell's Gully and continued up the snow above. The weather was terrible, with temperature of -20°F and wind up to 100 mph. Near the top of the Pinnacle, the two dug a snow hole to take shelter. The next day they attempted to rappel but were forced to abandon their rope (presumably it was stuck), and they tried to continue down on foot. Both fell to their deaths. Autopsies showed both had frozen hands and feet before their desperate attempt to descend.

Especially for newcomers to the mountain, a conservative approach is recommended. Conditions above tree line are always much worse than down in the forest. Turn back *before* things get really bad.

Before and during a trip to Mt. Washington, climbers and skiers can benefit from many information sources: real-time observations from the staffed observatory at the summit; Forest Service snow rangers who write a daily avalanche forecast and patrol the mountain in winter and spring; the caretakers at the Appalachian Mountain Club and Harvard Mountaineering Club huts; and a volunteer ski patrol. Good information is available—it's up to climbers to seek it out and make prudent decisions.

Many of the factors that make Mt. Washington so hazardous also make this an attractive place to learn the skills needed for much higher mountains. The best way to accumulate such knowledge is to climb or ski with experienced mentors. If you don't have access to friends with these skills, consider hiring one of the many professional guides in the area—it's an investment that will make the most of your time on one of North America's great peaks.

Dougald MacDonald, editor of this publication, learned winter mountaineering on Mt. Washington. Dan Cousins dug into the databases to produce the statistics for this article. Frank Carus, the lead snow ranger and director of the Mount Washington Avalanche Center, provided invaluable suggestions and feedback.

The accident scene on an unnamed peak in the Hidden Mountains. (1) Location of John and Alissa at the time of the fall. (2) Emmett's position. (3) Sarah's belay stance. The face is about 1,500 feet high. *Courtesy of Alissa Doherty*

ALASKA

FALL ON ROCK | Loose Rock
Lake Clark National Park, Hidden Mountains

Four climbers set out to explore the little-known Hidden Mountains in Lake Clark National Park in June. Their goal was to make first ascents of peaks in this remote region by climbing rock routes in single-push style. The day of the accident, the climbers had split into two parties, opting to climb neighboring ridgelines on the same peak. With a two-day window of stable weather, they each planned to ascend approximately 1,500 feet of class 4 and 5 terrain to the summit. Both parties carried Garmin inReach devices, making satellite texts possible.

On the evening of June 23, Emmett Lyman, 40, was 150 feet from his belayer, leading a pitch of approximately 5.7, around 800 feet above the start of the route. At 8 p.m., his belayer, Sarah Keyes, heard sizable rockfall and an inaudible reaction from Emmett. Sarah felt the rope tighten, presumably arresting Emmett's fall. She could not see Emmett but tried to initiate verbal communication and received no response.

After approximately 10 minutes, Sarah contacted the other members of the party, Alissa Doherty and John Gassel, via inReach. Alissa and John were 300 to 400 feet above and to the left of the injured party and immediately began a traverse and descent in an attempt to reach him. Meanwhile, Sarah initiated the team's emergency response plan by contacting Global Rescue and the expedition's emergency contact. She tied off the brake strand of the belay rope to free her hands but did not move or attempt to transfer the loaded rope to the anchor, out of concern that moving Emmett might cause additional rockfall or injury.

While making their descent, Alissa and John established visual and verbal communication with Emmett, who was unconscious but responsive to verbal stimulation.

EMERGENCY PLANNING: A CASE STUDY

For parties climbing in remote locations, the following information may be helpful in preparing for emergencies. Below is a list of actions we felt were important to the success of our rescue (see report at left) in Lake Clark National Park:

    (1) We had a safety plan that we distributed to several key contacts, including a safety coordinator at home. The following information was included in our safety plan:

- Designated primary emergency contact
- Local rescue contact information
- Global Rescue contact information
- Other emergency contacts, including pilots and climbers familiar with our climbing area
- Next of kin contact information
- Itinerary, proposed objectives, and potential hazards
- Gear carried by each climber and colors of gear/clothing
- Communication procedure for scenarios of search, rescue, and loss of life
- Climber medical conditions, health insurance, and rescue insurance information

    (2) We carried two inReach devices, which were pretested with our emergency contacts and preprogrammed with other important contacts.

    (3) We purchased supplemental rescue insurance through Global Rescue, which covered the high cost of Emmett's medical transport from Anchorage to Boston.

    (4) We participated in wilderness medical training shortly before the expedition.

    (5) We climbed as teams of two on nearby objectives, so assistance was near in case of emergency.

    (6) We waited for a two-day window of stable weather.

While we felt our safety preparation was adequate, we learned some things that would have been of use during the rescue. Here is a list of takeaways:

    (1) Despite the 24/7 daylight in Alaska at summer solstice, a headlamp would have been helpful to mark our location for rescuers. We used cell phone flashlights for signaling, which risked killing their batteries quickly.

    (2) We forgot our first-aid kit in camp and wished we had access to our Reflexcell blanket, which can be used for warmth and stabilization of patients.

    (3) In Alaska, direct initial contact with the Alaska Rescue Coordination Center (AKRCC) rather than Global Rescue will expedite assistance. This is a regionally specific takeaway—Global Rescue may be the optimal first contact in some scenarios, particularly outside of the United States. And Global Rescue should always be notified as soon as possible after an accident to ensure proper coverage.

    (4) In addition to using the Garmin inReach device for text communications, we should have used the SOS button on the device to transmit our location to as many rescue organizations as possible. (*Source: Alissa Doherty.*)

Realizing they would be unable to reach him directly, they descended to the anchor where Sarah was belaying, reaching this point at approximately 1:45 a.m.

At this time, the climbers heard an HH-60 Pave Hawk helicopter responding to their distress call, piloted by rescuers from Elmendorf Air Force Base's 210th Rescue Squadron. A thick fog obscured the peak, and the climbers were unable to establish visual contact with the helicopter. After an initial search, the helicopter dropped off three pararescue specialists at the climbers' base camp and departed to refuel.

During this time, Alissa belayed John up the rock to reach Emmett. John built an anchor above the gear that had arrested Emmett's fall and rappelled to him. He confirmed their assumption of head and neck trauma, covered Emmett with warm layers, and continued communicating with him while waiting for the helicopter to return.

At the anchor below, Alissa and Sarah established visual and verbal communication with the pararescue team in base camp, and they relayed the climbers' location to the pilots. After two stalled attempts to navigate in thick fog, the helicopter retrieved the pararescue team and started upward toward the injured climber.

Once in position, a pararescueman descended via hoist line, and John helped the rescuer reach the cliff. The line was attached to the injured climber's harness. Due to the helicopter's proximity to the cliff and Emmett's suspended position, spine stabilization was not possible. Emmett was hoisted into the helicopter at approximately 5 a.m., and rescuers began immediate medical treatment. He was flown to a hospital in Anchorage and was in surgery by 6 a.m.

The injured climber survived the accident and evacuation, having sustained two fractured vertebrae, spinal cord injury, closed head injury with associated traumatic brain injury, and an open fracture of his right arm. Sarah, Alissa, and John descended via rappel and returned to base camp at approximately 10 a.m. on June 24. They flew out the next day.

ANALYSIS

The injured climber had placed adequate gear (approximately 10 pieces in 150 feet), and his fall was arrested by the last piece he placed (a medium-sized nut). The fall distance was 20 to 30 feet. He was climbing within his technical ability and was wearing a helmet, which was lost when he received trauma to the head.

We believe that loose rock was responsible for the accident. Emmett likely weighted a loose or broken block, which in turn dislodged other rocks while also causing him to fall. A similar accident might be avoided by selecting objectives with high-quality rock or by retreating when loose rock is encountered.

This rescue was extremely well coordinated and executed. We were extraordinarily fortunate to receive specialized helicopter assistance within 10 hours of the accident. This expediency was unusual, given our remote location, and should not be counted on in any circumstances. In our case, light winds and a brief clearing of the fog on the mountain, along with efficient decision-making within the Alaska Rescue Coordination Center (AKRCC), were critical to the speed of the operation.

We owe deep gratitude to the AKRCC and the pilots and pararescue specialists from the 210th, 211th, and 212th squadrons at Elmendorf Air Force Base. Staff Sergeant Adam Brister was nominated for the Airman's Medal in recognition of his heroism during the rescue. (*Source: Alissa Doherty.*)

LEADER FALL ON ICE

Denali National Park, West Kahiltna Peak

At 9:42 a.m. on April 14, rangers were notified about an injured climber by a local air taxi service that had received a text from the climbing team's Garmin inReach device. The team of three reported that one climber had broken his right leg while attempting a new route on the west face of West Kahiltna Peak, at approximately 9,600 feet. Subsequent text messages confirmed that the 34-year-old male patient had sustained an open lower leg fracture during a 10- to 15-meter fall on ice while leading the third roped pitch of the line.

Favorable conditions in the mountain range enabled a helicopter reconnaissance flight and full scene assessment prior to patient evacuation. Rangers located the patient and teammates on an exposed snow and ice slope directly beneath a vertical rock face.

At 1:47 p.m., the rescue team landed at a staging area at 8,000 feet on the Kahiltna Glacier, and the helicopter was configured for a short-haul extraction using a 200-foot line. One mountaineering ranger functioned as the short-haul rescuer while another served as safety officer from the landing zone with a full view of the operation. Due to the steepness of the terrain and the potential for rockfall, the ranger remained on the short-haul line while assessing and packaging the patient, in order to expedite an extraction if required.

At 2:22 p.m., the ranger and patient landed back at the staging site, where the patient assessment was completed prior to loading into the helicopter. The patient was transported to Talkeetna in a full-body vacuum splint for both comfort and to stabilize the injury. The team landed in Talkeetna at 3:15 p.m., and the climber was transferred to ground ambulance for further treatment at a local hospital. (*Source: Denali Mountaineering Rangers.*)

The site of an accident on West Kahiltna Peak is shown, three pitches up a new route on the west face. The patient, who had a lower-leg fracture, was flown from the face in a short-haul helicopter mission. *Nik Mirhashemi*

ANALYSIS

This was a highly skilled team pushing into uncharted terrain on a difficult route (later rated AI5+ R M6+ C1). The leader fell when a bulge of rotten ice disintegrated. His fall was held by a screw, but any long fall on ice has the potential to cause serious injury. With the patient safely evacuated to the hospital, his two partners returned to finish the new route and later said the third pitch, where the patient fell, was the crux of the climb. (*Source: The Editors.*)

AVALANCHE | Proceeded Despite Hazardous Conditions
Denali National Park, West Fork of Ruth Glacier, Reality Ridge

In the early afternoon on May 3, a group of three ski mountaineers departed their base camp in the west fork of the Ruth Glacier. This was the first day of clearing following a storm that had lasted more than a week. Their objective was to climb and then ski an east-facing couloir on Denali's Reality Ridge. According to interviews with the team, as the skiers neared the top of the couloir, they began to have concerns about the snow stability. The preceding storm had deposited six feet of new snow in the area.

The team decided to stop their ascent, cross the couloir to a spot where they could put on their skis, and begin their descent. During this transition, a 31-year-old male in the group triggered an avalanche and was swept approximately 1,800 feet down the chute. The skier finally stopped at the bottom of the couloir, fortunately on top of the snow. Although he did not report losing consciousness during this accident, he sustained significant injuries. His partners, who were above him at the time of the avalanche, witnessed the entire event and were able to descend to his location.

Following a brief assessment, the team contacted their air taxi service via satellite phone and began to assist their injured partner back to camp. At 5:45 p.m., NPS rangers were notified of the incident and began planning for a rescue. Operations were streamlined due to direct satellite communications with the skiers, who provided frequent updates on the patient's progress toward camp and current medical condition.

Mountaineering rangers departed Talkeenta by helicopter and made contact with the patient at 7:09 p.m. Once back in Talkeetna, the patient was transferred to an ambulance at 7:47 p.m. and taken to a local hospital. He had suffered a dislocated left shoulder, a fractured jaw, a large chin laceration, and large contusions on the right thigh and right elbow.

ANALYSIS

May 3 was a single day of clearing weather between two large storm systems, lasting eight days and six days, respectively. During each of these storms, significant snowfall accumulated in the Alaska Range, raising the potential for natural and human-triggered avalanches. Although anyone would be eager to get out of the tent and climb or ski after an extended storm, it is paramount to remain vigilant to one's avalanche assessment and safe travel practices, regardless of the external pressures and the human factors that influence decision-making.

This party's decision to carry a satellite phone with them on the climb—and not simply stow the phone at base camp—facilitated a swift and effective rescue. (*Source: Denali Mountaineering Rangers.*)

FALL ON SNOW | Inadequate Protection
Denali National Park, Denali, West Buttress Route

Two climbers were ascending Denali's West Buttress at approximately 16,500 feet when they fell off the north side of the ridge (opposite the well-traveled route from the 14,200-foot camp). The fall occurred at 3:30 p.m. on May 20. The 29-year-old female and 27-year-old male climbers were roped together at the time of the fall,

but with hard surface snow conditions and without any protection clipped between them, they were unable to arrest their fall. They slid about 1,000 feet and into a crevasse on the Peters Glacier.

A guided climbing team witnessed this incident and made the initial report to NPS rangers stationed at 14,200-foot camp. In addition, one of the fallen climbers was able to signal for help with a personal locator beacon (PLB), which relayed their location at approximately 15,800 feet to both the Alaska Rescue Coordination Center and NPS personnel in Talkeetna.

An NPS ranger patrol descending from 17,200-foot camp on the West Buttress responded to the site of the initial fall. Due to the convexity of the terrain below and deteriorating weather, the rescue team could not see the climbers. They decided

Aerial view of Denali, showing approximate locations of (1) the crevasse into which two climbers slid on May 20, (2) the West Buttress, and (3) the 14,200-foot camp. *NPS Photo*

to return to 14,200-foot camp to prepare for a rescue with more personnel and equipment and to wait for more favorable weather. Multiple contingency plans were drafted in Talkeetna and on the mountain to accommodate rescuer safety in the dynamic weather conditions on the upper mountain. A rescue attempt by helicopter that evening turned around due to high winds and poor visibility.

Early on May 21, as ground rescue teams started toward the fixed lines that gain the West Buttress, they encountered the male patient limping into 14,200-foot camp with an injured knee. During the night, despite his injury, he had climbed back over the West Buttress and descended the fixed lines toward 14,200-foot camp. He reported that his climbing partner was alert and stable but injured and non-ambulatory in the crevasse that had stopped their fall.

A ground rescue team and the NPS helicopter team arrived at the injured patient's location at nearly the same time. She was assessed, immobilized for suspected spinal injuries, and extracted via short-haul back to 14,200-foot camp. After a flight to Talkeetna, she was transferred to an Anchorage hospital via air ambulance for treatment of cervical spine fractures. The patient's climbing partner was evacuated by helicopter the following day due to his unstable knee injury.

ANALYSIS

Roped glacier travel can provide a false sense of security. Failure to adapt fall protection methods to the current surface conditions has been the cause of many accidents. This is especially true when the surface becomes too firm for effective self-arrest. In softer snow conditions, where self-arresting is possible, solid footwork and using a mountaineering axe may be sufficient protection. As the surface hardens or transitions to ice, running protection (e.g. pickets or ice screws) is required to arrest a falling team member. The transition from soft to hard footing may be subtle, and conservative risk management strategies should be employed. The icy and rocky terrain of the West Buttress ridge is a location that requires running protection to effectively arrest a fall. (*Source: Denali Mountaineering Rangers.*)

AVALANCHE

Denali National Park, Mt. Hunter, Mini-Moonflower

On May 20, Britt Ruegger, 34, and I (age 29) were climbing the Mini-Moonflower Route when a debris avalanche swept the route and hit us as we were rappelling. We'd arrived at KIA (Kahiltna International Airport) on May 8 and proceeded to log some tent time during mixed weather. We climbed the first three or four pitches of the Mini-Moonflower on May 14 but bailed due to building snow. On May 20 we set out to give it another go.

In base camp that morning there was a trace of new snow, but by the time we were about 30 minutes from the base of the route we observed a foot of fresh snow, likely due to micro-orographic effects and temperature differences. I was a bit uneasy about how much new snow had fallen, but the weather didn't seem bad that day, and no new snow was forecast until the afternoon, which would give us time to climb most of the route.

Looking down the Mini-Moonflower Route at the stance where a climber was hit by an avalanche during a rappel descent, knocking him off the stance and breaking his arm. *Courtesy of Jared Drapala*

At the base of the climb I felt some apprehension, but sometimes you don't know until you go. We set off, swapping leads up eight or nine pitches. As we got within a pitch or two of the ridgeline, we decided to pull the plug because it seemed like the weather was turning.

We began to rappel. Above the crux pitch, we threaded the ropes through an in situ V-thread anchor and backed that up with an ice screw. I rappelled over the crux and down to the belay stance I had used on the way up, located in a semi-protected nook. At this point, since I still had more rope available, I had the choice to build a thread there or continue down. I continued another 10 to 15 meters to an angled shelf, making the rappel about 40 to 45 meters. I built a two-screw and quad anchor at the semi-hanging stance and clipped in with my tether. It was around 8:30 p.m. As I was preparing to pull the ropes out of my rappel device, I heard a rumble and looked up to see an avalanche headed at me. I grabbed the anchor and hoped for the best.

The avalanche pummeled me and knocked me off the stance. After it had passed and I got back on my feet, I realized something was wrong. When I reached up to finish removing the ropes from my device, my left hand wouldn't move up to meet my right. Either something carried by the slide or the force of being knocked off my stance had broken my left humerus at mid-shaft. Luckily, my partner was only dusted by the avalanche.

I placed my left wrist in a climbing sling and we continued our descent, which had its own challenges, including a stuck rope. While my partner solved that problem, I activated the SOS on his Garmin inReach device, 30 or 40 minutes after the avalanche. Once we reached the glacier, the NPS helicopter shuttled us to base camp, and in the evening I was flown to Talkeetna and a waiting ambulance. I had surgery later that night.

ANALYSIS

We don't know what caused the avalanche above us, but we hadn't adhered to the old adage of waiting at least a day after a storm to let the slopes shed snow, and perhaps we were threading the needle in regard to the weather pattern. We didn't really get much sleep the night before, which may have contributed to missing or not paying enough attention to telltale signs during the approach.

Although we both were carrying Garmin inReach devices, in the debrief with the NPS rangers we learned that, since we were so close to Kahiltna base, carrying a Talkabout-style radio would have allowed direct comms with the rangers at base camp. (*Source: Jared Drapala.*)

Editor's note: The Denali mountaineering rangers' report about this incident stated, "This team exhibited exemplary self-sufficiency in both the initial care and rescue of the injured climbing partner."

SEVERE ALTITUDE ILLNESS | Two Contrasting Cases
Denali National Park, Denali, West Buttress Route

On June 25, a 59-year-old male from a guided expedition descended from 17,200-foot camp with high altitude pulmonary edema (HAPE). This climber had spent two nights at that elevation until his shortness of breath and wet lung sounds became overwhelming. After a night of treatment and monitoring at 14,200-foot camp, the patient was able to self-evacuate with his team on June 26. This case highlights the benefits of immediate descent for patients exhibiting signs and symptoms of severe altitude illness—the benefits of descending often outweigh medical treatments.

Conversely, on May 22, a 40-year-old male who began experiencing signs and symptoms of severe altitude illness still continued his ascent to 14,200-foot camp. The patient reported to teammates that he was experiencing shortness of breath at rest, a productive cough, and a severe headache. Once at 14,200-foot camp, the climber continued to deteriorate throughout the night. Starting on May 23, NPS rangers treated him for both HAPE and high altitude cerebral edema (HACE) for the next 24 hours. When his condition failed to improve, he was evacuated via NPS helicopter on May 24.

ANALYSIS

Continuing to ascend while experiencing even mild acute mountain sickness (AMS) almost guarantees a worsening illness. AMS typically resolves by remaining at the current elevation until the climber is feeling better. Immediate descent is the recommended treatment for all patients suffering from any severe altitude illness.

When a patient is experiencing severe altitude sickness, it may prove difficult to distinguish between HAPE and HACE, and the two illnesses can be occurring simultaneously. In these cases, it is prudent to treat for both ailments throughout the course of care or until one of the ailments resolves. (See "Essentials: High Altitude Illness" in ANAC 2016, also available at publications.americanalpineclub.org.) Above all other treatment options, immediate descent should be the priority for these patients. (*Source: Denali Mountaineering Rangers.*)

SEVERE ALTITUDE ILLNESS | HAPE and HACE
Denali National Park, Denali, West Buttress Route

At 10:06 p.m. on June 1, NPS rangers were notified via Garmin inReach that a climber near the summit ridge appeared to be suffering from severe altitude illness. Other climbers in the vicinity had administered two doses of dexamethasone, a steroid used to treat HACE, in hopes the climber could continue his descent. The severity of the patient's condition made a ground rescue from 17,200-foot camp impractical.

The NPS helicopter was flown from Talkeetna just after midnight on June 2. A mountaineering ranger was picked up at 14,200-foot camp for a reconnaissance, and the climbing team of three, including the patient, was located at approximately 18,500 feet on the West Buttress Route, near Zebra Rocks. The helicopter returned to 14,200-foot camp, where a rescue basket was rigged to the short-haul line. The pilot extracted the patient and returned to 14,200-foot camp at 12:45 a.m. The patient and an NPS volunteer medic then flew to Talkeetna.

ANALYSIS
The difficulty of rescue at high altitudes should always underscore one's risk assessment and decision-making. As soon as weather, climbing conditions, or a climber's health deteriorate high on the mountain, climbers should retreat. The likelihood of a rescue often diminishes with each step higher in elevation. (*Source: Denali Mountaineering Rangers.*)

ALTITUDE-RELATED EVACUATION AT 17,200 FEET: *In addition to the altitude illness cases described above, a 47-year-old male climber was evacuated from 17,200-foot camp on May 31 with signs and symptoms of both HAPE and HACE. The team reported that they had ascended to that high camp from base camp (7,200 feet) in only four days. A gradual ascent profile is key in the prevention of all types of altitude illness.*

FALL ON SKIS | Skiing With Loaded Sled
Denali National Park, Kahiltna Glacier

On the evening of June 3, two climbers were descending toward base camp on skis. One of the climbers fell after being pulled to the side by his gear sled. The 51-year-old climber reported feeling and hearing a popping sensation in his left knee during the fall. The two were able to continue their descent to 7,800-foot camp, about 5.5 miles away from Kahiltna base, before the swelling and pain became too much for continued travel.

The following morning, the climbing team notified NPS personnel in camp that the patient could no longer bear weight on his leg. At approximately 7:30 p.m. on June 4, once

inclement weather cleared, a moun-
tainccring ranger and pilot evacuated
the patient by helicopter to Talkeetna.

ANALYSIS

Denali provides the rare–and often
dreaded–opportunity to ski between
camps, roped up for glacier travel,
carrying heavy packs and towing an
expedition sled. These skills are often
ncw to climbers on the mountain. If
possible, practice before your expedition, and then take extreme care
while skiing with loads. Many climbing seasons have ended early due to
injuries sustained during these activities. (*Source: Denali Mountaineering
Rangers.*)

Descending with a loaded sled below 14,200-foot
camp on Denali's West Buttress Route, with Mt. Foraker
in the background. *Brody Leven*

FROSTBITE

Denali National Park, Denali, West Buttress Route

On June 4, a guided group summited Denali via the West Buttress climbing route.
The lead guide reported that "...temperatures were between -10°F and -20°F. Once
above Denali Pass, winds were estimated at a consistent 15 to 20 mph, with occasional
gusts of 25 to 30 mph." These observations were consistent with other climber and
NPS ranger reports that day. At 10 p.m., the wind increased and visibility decreased
on the upper mountain while the guided team was descending the peak.

At 2:30 a.m. on June 5, mountaineering rangers at 17,200-foot camp were notified that two climbers on this guided expedition had returned to camp with frostbite injuries sustained during their summit climb and needed medical assistance.
The rangers assessed both patients and deemed that one required urgent evacuation. The 53-year-old male had deep frostbite injuries to all ten fingers, all ten toes,
and his nose. The patient believed that most of the frostbite occurred during the slow
descent to camp; he reported that his fingers had frozen when he removed his mittens
to manipulate the carabiners on snow pickets. The NPS team worked throughout the
night to rewarm the affected extremities on both patients while awaiting flyable weather.

At 9:37 a.m., the NPS helicopter flew to high camp and evacuated the 53-year-old
patient to base camp, where he was transferred to an air ambulance and ultimately
transferred directly to the frostbite specialists at the University of Utah Burn Center
in Salt Lake City for advanced treatment. Subsequent reports revealed that this climber
had nearly all of the frostbitten tissue amputated during the course of his care.

Following the evacuation of the first patient, the second patient, a 31-year-old
male, was also flown from high camp due to deep frostbite injury on one of his feet.
The ranger team was concerned that this climber could not descend safely on the
frostbitten limb and opted to evacuatc in ordcr to prevent further injury.

ANALYSIS

Deep frostbite injuries often have long-term consequences. It is essential for climbers to actively rewarm body parts that become cold while traveling in alpine conditions. When environmental circumstances prevent the rewarming of these body parts, climbers must seek shelter or descend to a more hospitable location to prevent further injury. Keep in mind that if a frozen body part is thawed, refreezing must be prevented, as this will increase the severity of the original injury. (*Source: Denali Mountaineering Rangers.*)

CARBON MONOXIDE POISONING

Denali National Park, Denali, West Buttress Route

On the evening of June 6, NPS rangers were alerted about a climber who was unresponsive and experiencing seizures in 14,200-foot camp. This 40-year-old male had been pulled from his tent when his climbing partner found him experiencing seizures while cooking in their tent during a storm. The responding mountaineering ranger and his team found the patient was initially responsive only to painful stimuli, but after 30 minutes of oxygen therapy he had returned to normal mental status.

DEALING WITH A DEADLY GAS

Carbon monoxide (CO) is a colorless and odorless gas that is produced after any fossil fuel is burned. Inside a tent or snow cave, especially one that has little to no ventilation, a dangerous buildup of the gas may result in poisoning or death. There have been at least three incidents of CO poisoning on Denali: two non-fatal incidents in 1985 and 2018, and one fatal incident in 1988.

The most common signs and symptoms of CO poisoning are headache, dizziness, weakness, upset stomach, vomiting, chest pain, and confusion. While easily recognizable, these signs and symptoms are similar to those of acute mountain sickness (AMS), and so the cause may not be immediately identified. Severe CO poisoning signs and symptoms are almost identical to high altitude cerebral and pulmonary edema (HACE, HAPE), with progressive confusion, ataxia, loss of consciousness (HACE), hypoxia, and shortness of breath (HAPE).

To avoid poisoning, attempt to cook outside or in a well-ventilated area such as a tent vestibule; if forced to cook inside, make sure there is plenty of ventilation. While cooking, keep your stove highly pressurized, avoid prolonged simmering, keep the flame blue (yellow flames tend to create more CO), use small diameter pans, and use white, pure fuels if possible. Carbon monoxide builds up more easily in low wind conditions.

If you begin to have the above signs and symptoms while cooking, immediately exit the tent. And if you or your climbing partner are concerned about CO buildup in your tent, just remember, "If in doubt, air it out!"

If available, supplemental oxygen will rapidly reverse symptoms of CO poisoning.

– R. Bryan Simon

Both this patient and his climbing partner, a 44-year-old male, were found to be suffering from carbon monoxide (CO) poisoning. The partner had exited their tent when "feeling off" and thus was able to alert others that his partner had become unresponsive.

Both of these patients required constant treatment and monitoring until the weather cleared two days later. At this time, both climbers were flown to town and taken to the hospital for further testing and treatment for acute and chronic CO poisoning. During their stay in the NPS medical tent, the patients received alternating treatment with supplemental oxygen and hyperbaric therapy in the Portable Altitude Chamber in hopes of expediting the removal of CO from their red blood cells.

ANALYSIS

Carbon monoxide poisoning is a life threat for mountaineers, especially when weather conditions force climbers to seek shelter while cooking. The outcome of this incident could have been catastrophic had one of the climbers not responded to his "unwell feeling" by exiting the tent for fresh air. The changes to a patient exposed to carbon monoxide can be subtle and often unrecognized by those exposed, as initially the signs and symptoms may mimic the effects of altitude or general unwellness. Adequate ventilation should always be the priority when cooking in an enclosed space such as a tent. (*Source: Denali Mountaineering Rangers.*)

2018 DENALI SEASON SUMMARY: *In total, mountaineering rangers and patrol volunteers treated 30 patients during the 2018 season. Sixteen patients required helicopter evacuation. There were no climbing-related fatalities in 2018, the first time this has happened since 2003.*

ROCKFALL | Impacted by Tumbling Rock
Hayes Range, Mt. Skarland

On May 12, I (female, age 35) was scrambling up Mt. Skarland (10,315 feet) in the eastern Hayes Range when a boulder, approximately two feet in diameter, was dislodged by a climber above and struck my left hand. I suffered a hemorrhaging crush injury and near complete avulsion of the hand, which necessitated applying a tourniquet in the field. I was climbing with four alpinists—Katie Bono, Ben Chapman, Alexander Lee, and Alan Shanoski—all of whom participated in extracting me from the steep shale and snow slope.

As my bleeding became controlled with the tourniquet, the team activated the SOS on a Garmin inReach and then communication was established with Alaska State Troopers via a satellite phone. We assigned clear roles to each climber and initiated a plan for descent, taking into account the safety of each person and the resources available to us.

A medevac helicopter arrived on scene three to four hours after the initial rockfall. The helicopter was only able to land safely at the base of the mountain, 1,500 feet below, so we had to descend a mixed scree and steep snow slope to the base. The skills and teamwork of the group made it possible to descend through a series of eight or nine rope lowers. An incredibly skilled pilot flew us out with no daylight to spare, and the work of my team and the emergency responders, coupled with extensive trauma training in my personal career, ultimately saved my life. I was flown to a hospital in Fairbanks, where I was stabilized, and then by air ambulance to the nearest level one trauma center in Seattle, where I began a series of complicated surgical repairs to my hand. (*Source: Ilana Jesse.*)

ANALYSIS

Traveling steep terrain in a group increases the hazard anytime a rock is knocked loose. Moving one at a time through suspect areas, while the remaining climbers wait out of the fall zone, can minimize the hazard.

This team's ample preparation and multiple systems for communicating with rescuers prevented a bad accident from having a more serious outcome. (*Source: The Editors.*)

FATAL FALL DURING DESCENT
Juneau Icefield, Mendenhall Towers

On March 5, in early afternoon, Ryan Johnson and Marc-André Leclerc reached the summit of the Main Tower (6,910') in the Mendenhall Towers massif, after completing the first ascent of the north face. The pair started down the east ridge and then began rappelling the Fourth Gully, a steep cleft leading down to the glacier to the north. During this descent, an unknown event caused the men to fall down the gully and into a crevasse. Searchers later spotted ropes in the crevasse, and a hovering helicopter with Recco search technology determined the victims must be located inside the crevasse. A recovery was not possible.

ANALYSIS

It's unknown what caused the two men to fall, but searchers and friends believe they

After climbing the north face of Main Tower in the Mendenhall Towers (shown), two climbers descended the left skyline ridge and then started down the very steep couloir dropping from the saddle. *Kieran Brownie*

likely were hit by something from above, such as rockfall or an avalanche. Descending in the afternoon, the warmest part of the day, might have increased this possibility.

Although weather prevented searchers from finding the climbers' location with any hope of rescuing them alive, the Recco reflector installed on at least one item of their clothing or equipment permitted searchers to pinpoint their location. Alpinists are reminded of the value of carrying avalanche transceivers or similar location technology in glaciated or avalanche-prone terrain. In addition to possibly saving one's own life, it can make searchers' job much safer and more effective, possibly offering some comfort to survivors. (*Source: The Editors.*)

ARIZONA

LEDGE FALL | Failure to Clip Bolt, Inexperience
Flagstaff Area, The Pit

In the early afternoon on April 12, Person 1 (female, age 23) fell about 30 feet while leading Sunshine Daydream, a 5.7 sport climb at the Pit. Person 1 had ascended approximately 20 feet to a small ledge and then continued up. She was attempting to clip the third bolt above the ledge, and the belayer had paid out slack for Person 1 to make the clip, when she lost her grip and fell approximately 30 feet onto the ledge.

Person 1 sustained a head injury, thoracic spine injuries, and a pelvic injury. Rescuers packaged her in a litter and lowered her to the bottom of the canyon, from which a litter team carried her out of the canyon to a waiting ambulance.

On this climb, Person 1 was leading outdoors for the first time. (She had previously led climbs in an indoor climbing gym.) Person 1 was not wearing a helmet. The belayer, Person 2 (age 18), had five years of experience.

ANALYSIS
This route is rated 5.7 and has been described as a good route for first leads, with eight bolts and good clipping stances. The potential complicating factor was the intermediate ledge, which provided a hazard if a clip was missed and the climber fell. The other hazard was the high wind, which may not have affected the climber's ability to ascend the route but could have made verbal communication difficult between the climber and the belayer. A helmet may have mitigated some of the injuries sustained by Person 1. (*Source: Aaron Dick, Coconino County Sheriff's Office.*)

EDITOR'S NOTE: *Ledge falls are one of the hazards that new climbers generally won't encounter in a gym setting but frequently find outdoors—especially on easier routes like this one. When transitioning to outdoor routes, climbers must learn to judge such hazards and avoid falls that might be consequential. Seek a balanced position before attempting a difficult clip, and don't pull up slack unless you're in balance. Practice downclimbing to a rest position to recover when a clip can't be made the first time. A homemade or purchased "stiff draw," such as the Kong Panic quickdraw, may allow shorter climbers to clip out-of-reach bolts.*

GROUND FALL | Inadequate Equipment, Inexperience
Flagstaff Area, The Pit

On September 9, at 1:20 p.m., Coconino County Sheriff's Office and other agencies responded to a report of a 12-year-old male, Person 1, who took a 20-foot ground fall while lead climbing. Upon arrival, responders found Person 1 at the base of Microwave, a short 5.11 sport climb. He had lost consciousness for approximately one minute and had shown decorticate posturing immediately after the fall, suggesting a possible brain injury. He also had a fractured right wrist. He was packaged in a litter and transported to Flagstaff Medical Center for treatment.

An investigation revealed this was the party's first climb of the day. Starting up the route, Person 1 clipped single carabiners to each bolt, with the rope clipped directly through them (no quickdraws). Person 1 had clipped the first two bolts with these carabiners and was in the process of clipping the third when he fell. The carabiners clipped to the first two bolts both broke, resulting in the subject landing at the base of the climb.

ANALYSIS

Person 1 had climbed outside a few times prior to this incident, but most of his experience was in a climbing gym. He had purchased the carabiners that broke from Amazon.

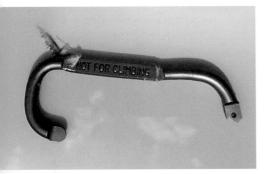

Two of these snap link–style carabiners broke in a fall. The carabiners were clearly marked "Not For Climbing," but the warning had been covered with tape. *Aaron Dick*

com. They were stamped "Not For Climbing" along the spine; however, the spine on each carabiner had been wrapped with athletic tape, making it difficult to inspect the equipment. The other members of the party (both adults with some climbing experience) had not double-checked the gear before it was used.

Carabiners that are not rated for climbing activity should never be used for climbing, nor should the strength rating or other safety information on equipment be covered up. Person 1 was wearing a helmet when he fell, which may have prevented additional injury. (*Source: Aaron Dick, Coconino County Sheriff's Office.*)

RAPPEL ERROR | Uneven Ropes, No Stopper Knots
Flagstaff Area, Oak Creek Overlook

On July 2 a climber took a 15- to 20-foot ground fall while on rappel at the Oak Creek Canyon overlook. The climber sustained a back injury. The climber was rappelling approximately 75 feet from the top of the cliff to the start of the route Burnt Buns (5.8). Prior to the rappel, he did not ensure that both rope ends were even or on the ground. When he was approximately 20 feet above the bottom of the route, the end of one strand of the rope passed through the device, causing an uncontrolled descent to the ground. He was wearing a helmet and did not sustain any head injury.

ANALYSIS

The climber, who had decades of climbing experience, and his two younger and inexperienced companions did not ensure that both rope ends reached the ground. Some climbers skip the step of tying stopper knots in the rope ends for relatively short rappels like this one, but a solid knot would have prevented the shorter strand from slipping through the rappel device. Although rappelling to approach these climbs is common, a climber's trail also provides access. If at least one member of the party had walked to the base, he or she could have ensured that both rope ends were on the ground as well as provided a fireman's belay for backup. (*Source: Aaron Dick, Coconino County Sheriff's Office.*)

FALL FROM ANCHOR | Inadequate Anchor
Flagstaff Area, Oak Creek Overlook

On November 10, person 1 (female, 34) fell 40 to 60 feet from the top of the Oak Creek Vista overlook to the rocky trail below, suffering numerous serious injuries. An unaffiliated witness stated that he observed her climb to the top of the wall and then move the rope to another anchor to prepare a different line for climbing. The witness observed that this second anchor was a rope or cord that had been left in place around a boulder. He observed Person 1 rotate the cordage around the boulder and then thread the rappel rope into her descending device, and then fall as she lifted the attached device to clip it to her harness. The rope, belay device, and carabiner were located on the ground near Person 1, corroborating the witness' account.

Due to the difficult access to the accident site, a helicopter short-haul operation was conducted to transfer the patient to the parking lot above the climbs, where she was transferred to an air ambulance. She had a spinal injury, head trauma, collapsed lungs, and other internal injuries and fractures.

ANALYSIS
Although it wasn't possible to determine the exact cause of Person 1's fall, it seems likely that the cord around the boulder that formed the intended anchor either pulled up and over the boulder, broke, or came untied as Person 1 attempted to rig her rappel. Person 1 appeared not to have constructed the anchor, and it is unknown if she inspected the cordage adequately prior to using it. An adjacent juniper tree might have offered less risk of anchor failure compared to a sling around a smooth, rounded boulder. The climber also could have anchored temporarily to the tree for edge protection while she worked in the exposed space around the boulder anchor. (*Source: Coconino County Search and Rescue.*)

GROUND FALL | Protection Pulled Out
McDowell Mountains, Tom's Thumb

On November 28, a male climber, DS (21), was leading Succubus, a 5.10 trad finger crack. The crux of the climb is approximately 25 feet up, where you move right under a roof to reach a finger crack. DS placed what he felt was a solid 0.5 Black Diamond C4 and 0.1 Black Diamond X4 under the roof, then reached around the roof to place an insecure 0.3 C4 before committing to the finger crack. As DS continued, his foot slipped. His belayer, AO (female, 27), was ready for the catch, but all three pieces he had placed at the crux pulled and DS fell 30 feet, impacting the ground and breaking his right pinky toe, bruising his back, and hitting his head on a rock. DS was wearing a helmet. After about an hour of rest, he was able to self-rescue by hiking out and driving to a hospital.

ANALYSIS
DS had been climbing for less than a year, and his relative lack of experience placing gear played into the accident. His three takeaways were: 1) When protecting high-risk moves, take the time to make a secure placement before committing; 2) Use the correct gear (people familiar with the route recommended placing nuts as protection under the roof instead of cams; and 3) Always wear a helmet. (*Source: DS.*)

In the low-snow season on Shasta, long carries of injured climbers may require a dozen or more rescue personnel. *USFS Photo*

CALIFORNIA

MT. SHASTA ANNUAL SUMMARY
Mt. Shasta and Castle Crags Wilderness

In 2018 there were eight climbing-related accidents on Mt. Shasta. Four were due to falls on ice or snow, two were due to rockfall, and one was the result of glissading with crampons; little information is available about the eighth incident. In addition, there were numerous searches involving lost climbers (*see note below*). Despite a total of 20 search and rescue incidents on the mountain—well above the recent annual average—there were no fatalities in 2018.

On May 12, a female climber, age 32, fell and slid a reported 1,000 feet in Avalanche Gulch after lunging for a dropped cell phone to prevent it from sliding down the steep, firm slope. She suffered a fractured ankle and multiple scrapes and bruises. She was wearing crampons and had an ice axe. Gale-force winds and strong downdrafts on the mountain prevented a helicopter rescue, so rangers and volunteers brought her down Avalanche Gulch in a toboggan, a process taking many hours. This incident could have been easily prevented by focusing on the task at hand rather than multi-tasking in terrain with fall potential.

On May 14, a 65-year-old male climber was struck in the head by rockfall while descending Avalanche Gulch near the Heart. He had been wearing a helmet, but had taken it off to adjust the headband or liner when he was hit. The climber momentarily lost consciousness but was able to self-rescue. He suffered a two-inch scalp laceration to the back of his head.

An 18-year-old male attempted to glissade down the Avalanche Gulch on June 18 while wearing crampons. Near the Heart, his crampons stuck in the snow and he suffered a broken ankle. Rangers continually attempt to educate climbers regarding proper glissade technique—including never glissading with crampons—but each year this type of accident still occurs.

On June 23, a male climber (age unknown) fell an unknown distance in Avalanche Gulch. The climber was able to self-rescue with the help of his partners. He sustained major abrasions to his buttocks and back. A second accident on June 23 occurred on the west face. A novice male climber (mid-30s) fell approximately 1,500 feet after a slip while off-route; he attempted to self-arrest but lost control of his axe. His fall was witnessed by a Shasta Mountain Guides employee, who assisted the climber after the fall. The climber suffered a broken heel, a broken small toe, a sprained ankle, and an unspecified knee injury.

A 29-year-old male climber was climbing the Avalanche Gulch route early on the morning of June 30 when a large rock came tumbling over the Red Banks and struck the climber in the ankle, resulting in a short fall. The climber was unable to walk, and his ankle was slightly angulated, indicating a likely ankle fracture. His partners and other climbers improvised a litter with a closed-cell foam sleeping pad and various pieces of webbing and were able to self-rescue, dragging the injured climber down to Helen Lake. He was then loaded onboard an Army National Guard helicopter and transferred to a local medical facility.

On July 1, a 49-year-old male climber slipped while downclimbing through Red Banks. He fell approximately 200 feet and sustained facial lacerations and abrasions but no other significant injuries. He was able to continue his descent, along with his climbing partners, without issue. At the end of July, a female climber broke her leg at approximately 11,500 feet. Additional information is unknown, but it is presumed she fell.

ANALYSIS

Search and rescue incidents nearly doubled from the year before. That said, conditions on Shasta were never abnormally dangerous. Most incidents on the mountain involve either slips and falls on steep snow and failing to self-arrest or climbers getting lost. Learning to self-arrest and knowing how to navigate are essential skills for wilderness and mountaineering, not just on Shasta but anywhere in the world.

The rangers often talk about "mountain sense" to climbers. This is a hard topic to teach, but mountain sense involves making good decisions based on your personal and/or group knowledge, skills, and abilities. It's listening to that little voice in your head and forcing "summit fever" to the side when the conditions, weather, visibility, or the group's fitness and readiness aren't optimal. (*Source: Mt. Shasta and Castle Crags Wilderness 2018 Climbing Ranger Report.*)

Example of route-finding info marked on a climber's photo by rangers and texted back to the climbers to help them get back on track. *USFS Photo*

LOST CLIMBERS ON SHASTA: In addition to the incidents described above, there were seven cases in 2018 involving lost climbers. Climbers most often get off-route on the upper mountain, above around 12,500 feet. Avoid climbing into a whiteout or clouds, especially when unfamiliar with the terrain. Most climbers could avoid becoming lost with basic navigation tools and situational awareness, but too few climbers carry dedicated navigation tools of any sort. Smartphone mapping applications can work very well; a simple recommendation is to learn to use one of these apps and how to use your phone to provide lat/long coordinates to rescue personnel. An extra charge stick (battery) for your phone is a great idea too.

In 2018, there were three false alarms or accidental activations of Satellite Emergency Notification Devices (SEND devices), such as the Garmin inReach and SPOT Messenger. It is essential for climbers to secure these devices to prevent false alarms, which waste valuable resources that may be needed for actual emergencies. (*Source: Mt. Shasta and Castle Crags Wilderness 2018 Climbing Ranger Report.*)

LEDGE FALL | Inadequate Protection, Speed Climbing
Yosemite National Park, El Capitan, The Nose

On May 3, Hans Florine and a climbing partner started a climb of the Nose of El Capitan at approximately 7 a.m. Both are highly experienced. Florine has made over 100 ascents of the Nose and has held the speed record on the route; his partner had climbed El Cap multiple times, including speed ascents of the Nose with Florine. The two were planning to do the route in 10 to 12 hours.

At some point in the first half of the climb, the team dropped a gear sling that contained some of their smaller cams, leaving them with only a set of small nuts and Camalots 0.5 and larger. The two decided that it was reasonable to continue up the route, improvising in spots with the gear that they had.

On pace for a 12-hour time, the team arrived at the Pancake Flake (pitch 22) with Florine in the lead. To move quickly through such technical terrain, the team was "short fixing." This technique involves pulling up the excess rope at the end of a pitch and fixing it for the second to jumar. The leader then self-belays into the next pitch until he runs out of rope or his partner arrives at the anchor and puts the leader on a normal belay. This is an advanced speed climbing technique that saves time but can increase risk to the leader.

After climbing the initial hand crack on Pancake Flake, Florine arrived at Triangle Ledge, a stance that marks the start of a thin crack just before the next anchor. Not having the ideal gear for this section, Florine started up the corner, placing three small nuts and one cam. His next piece, a nut, failed when he weighted it. He fell approximately 20 feet, striking Triangle Ledge along the way, before the cam he had placed arrested his fall. He was still self-belaying at the time.

Both legs were injured in the fall (a pilon fracture in one leg and a shattered calcaneus in the other). The climbers were unable to rappel the route because of Florine's injuries. He pulled himself up onto Triangle Ledge and had already called 911 for help by the time his partner arrived at the anchor below.

Due to the non-life-threatening nature of the injuries as well as high winds, it was decided that a "top down" rescue was the safest option for accessing the patient. The plan was to shuttle the SAR team and gear to a landing site on top of El Cap using a helicopter. Then the decision to raise Florine to the top or lower him to the bottom would be made, based on environmental conditions at the time.

While talking to the SAR team on the phone, Florine asked about trying to rappel to a larger ledge where pain management would be easier. It was decided by both parties that rappelling to the Gray Ledges, about 300 to 400 feet below the site of the accident, was the best option.

By 7 p.m., rescuers had reached the climbers, and soon the decision was made to raise the patient to the summit. After being treated for pain and packaged into a litter, a long-hauling operation began, and at approximately 10 p.m., Florine and the two rescue team members arrived at the summit. (Florine's partner rappelled to the base of El Capitan.) The patient spent the night on top of the Nose with the SAR team, receiving medical care from paramedics. Early the next day, he was flown down to El Cap Meadow.

Yosemite rangers Brandon Latham (left) and Philip Johnson, having lowered from the top of El Capitan, arrive at Gray Ledges to retrieve Hans Florine (right). *Hans Florine*

ANALYSIS

Protect yourself over ledges. While a 20-foot fall in overhanging terrain or on a blank wall can present little risk, any ledge or protrusion can introduce serious consequences. If climbing above a ledge, place gear early and often.

Reassess risks during a climb. After dropping the gear sling with the smaller cams, the team could have chosen to turn around. Although both climbers were very knowledgeable about the terrain above, the loss of those pieces of protection greatly enhanced the seriousness of the upper part of the climb.

Speed climbing. Speed climbing techniques—and mindset—can put climbers at greater risk. Less gear, non-standard belay techniques, and haste add risk and consequences to already difficult climbs. (Source: *Yosemite National Park Climbing Rangers*.)

An interview with Hans Florine about this incident is featured in episode 30 of the Sharp End podcast.

LOWERING ERROR | Inexperience, No Stopper Knot
Yosemite Valley, Reed's Pinnacle

On May 7 two climbers headed to the route Lunatic Fringe (single-pitch 5.10c). The leader was fairly experienced (four to five years), and the belayer had about 1.5 years of experience. The two had climbed together the day before in the Valley. Lunatic Fringe was at the leader's limit for traditional lead climbing in the area, and he hung twice while on the route. After arriving at the anchors, the leader clipped in direct and then pulled his blue 65-meter rope up through the gear he had placed and dropped an end back down to the belayer. The leader then tagged up a second rope (green 60-meter). The climb is roughly 43 to 45 meters high and requires two ropes to rappel or top-rope.

Once the leader had hauled up the green line, he tied the ends together using a flat overhand with a backup. He rigged the knot on the side of the anchor that would allow the green line to be pulled to retrieve the two ropes. At this moment, the leader was perfectly set up to rappel to the ground safely. Instead, he tied a bight in the green rope approximately one meter below the joined ends and clipped this to his harness with a locking carabiner. (*Rock & Ice magazine reported that he had forgotten his rappel device and thus decided to lower instead of rappel.*) He unclipped from the anchor and asked the belayer to lower him with the blue rope that was threaded through the anchor; essentially he would be lowering on his single 65-meter lead rope. When the end of the blue rope reached the belayer, it passed through her tube-style device and the leader fell approximately 10 meters to the ground. He suffered numerous serious injuries.

ANALYSIS

Rappelling from these anchors with two ropes tied together is the preferred option. If the leader forgot his rappel device, he could have asked the belayer to tie it to a rope and then hauled it up. Instead, the leader switched plans to lower but did not have a good understanding of the consequences of his chosen method, nor did he and the belayer communicate clearly about the new plan. Despite the faulty lowering plan, closing the belay system still could have prevented the leader's ground fall. A knot was found at the end of the green line, but the blue rope (on which the leader effectively was lowering) had no stopper knot and was not tied to the belayer. (*Sources: Yosemite National Park Climbing Rangers and the Editors.*)

STRANDED ON DESCENT | Off-Route, Fatigue
Yosemite Valley, El Capitan, East Ledges

On two days in a row in early June, YOSAR responded to climbers stranded after failing to make their way down the East Ledges descent from the top of El Capitan, which requires a mix of rappelling and scrambling.

The first party had climbed the East Buttress route on June 2 and attempted to follow the "Option C" descent shown in the popular Supertopo guidebook. However, this descent requires two ropes to rappel and the team only had one. After one rappel, the party found a two-bolt rappel station and assumed they were at the correct location. They pulled their single line and committed to that descent. After rappelling again, they became stranded on a ledge.

The team had cell phone service and called YOSAR. Due to the late hour, they were instructed to wait on the ledge for rescue in the morning. Two YOSAR members responded to the East Ledges and assisted the party down.

Later that same day, two more East Buttress climbers were stranded on the East Ledges rappels. They had followed rock cairns and a faint climbers' trail leading toward the edge of El Capitan. At some point the team found a manzanita bush with webbing and rappel rings and began rappelling from that location. At the end of the first rappel, they found bolted rappel anchors at a ledge, which led them to believe they were on the standard rappel route.

After pulling their single 60-meter rope, one member of the party rappelled down 30 meters, only to find there were no more rappel stations on the blank face. He used prusiks to ascend the ropes to his partner, but the terrain above them was far beyond their ability to climb back up to the rim.

The next morning, two SAR-siters climbed up the East Ledges, located the two climbers, and gave them a tutorial on how to use ascending devices. The climbers then ascended a fixed rope with a belay from above.

ANALYSIS
The climbers involved were experienced in multi-pitch climbing, but had never descended off El Cap. They told SAR personnel that they were tired after climbing their routes and that haste played a big factor in these incidents. Slow down and think things through toward the end of the day. When fatigue has set in, it is easier to make mistakes.

When rappelling into unknown terrain, it is imperative to continuously analyze your situation. If you observe that you would be unable to climb back up the terrain you're rappelling, be certain you can continue down with the equipment you have before pulling the ropes above you. (When you commit to climbing with only one rope, your descent options are severely limited. If you are not familiar with a descent, consider bringing two ropes the first time. Even though guidebooks show a number of options for rappelling the East Ledges, only one option is possible with a single rope.) Often, leaving gear to create your own rappel anchors is a feasible option.

When continuing down is impossible, it's important to know the techniques for ascending ropes. The climber in the June 3 incident had these skills and was able to spend the night on a ledge as opposed to hanging at the end of a rope. (*Source: Yosemite National Park Climbing Rangers.*)

TWO GROUND FALLS | Inadequate Protection, Rope Severed
Yosemite Valley, El Capitan

Around 6 a.m. on the morning of June 2, Tim Klein, Kevin Prince, and Jason Wells started up El Capitan with the objective of climbing the Salathé Wall (VI 5.9 C2) in a day. All three were very familiar with the terrain. Klein had climbed El Capitan 108 times, Wells over 90 times, and Prince roughly 20 times. The full team had climbed together previously, including a one-day ascent of the Salathé four years prior. Additionally, Klein and Wells had an estimated 40 one-day ascents of the Salathé, including a sub-eight-hour ascent.

On the day of the accident, the trio's goal was not a speed record but simply to enjoy an in-a-day ascent, with Wells and Prince attempting to free climb the route. To be efficient, the team was short-fixing, an advanced climbing technique popular among speed climbers on El Capitan. This consists of the leader climbing a pitch, pulling up the slack, fixing the lead line for the follower, and then continuing either on self-belay or without a belay with the remainder of the available rope. The follower ascends the fixed lead line and upon arriving at the anchor places the leader back on a standard belay.

Because they were climbing as a team of three, the second climber was tagging (trailing) an additional rope behind him and fixing it at each belay anchor. The third climber then would self-belay on this rope using progress-capture devices (e.g., Micro Traxion).

Early that morning, around Triangle Ledge, the trio caught and passed a party

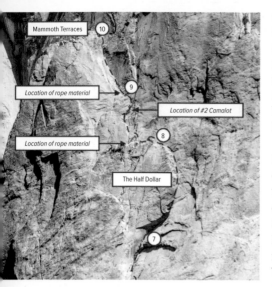

Mammoth Terraces — 10

Location of rope material — 9

Location of #2 Camalot

Location of rope material — 8

The Half Dollar

7

Area on the Salathé Wall where two men simul-climbing the ninth and tenth pitches fell to the ground when their rope severed. *NPS Photo*

attempting a multi-day ascent of Golden Gate. Wells was leading, Klein was second and ascending the lead line, and Prince was rope-soloing behind the other two using the second rope. Not far above Triangle Ledge is the Half Dollar chimney, followed by roughly 250 feet of 5.7 and easier terrain leading to the top of Mammoth Terraces.

Wells and Klein climbed through the Half Dollar and went out of sight of the others below. Klein yelled down to Prince that his rope was fixed, and Prince began climbing the Half Dollar. At approximately 8:05 a.m., while Prince was behind the Half Dollar and unable to view his climbing partners, something happened that caused Wells and Klein to fall. It is unknown which climber fell first.

A climber in the Golden Gate team who was positioned at the pitch seven anchor, in view of the area below Mammoth Terraces, saw Wells in mid-fall. The climber then heard Klein yell and saw him come into view, also falling. The climber said he saw the fall briefly arrested before the rope apparently failed. The two fell approximately 1,000 feet to the base of El Capitan.

Upon reaching the anchor above the Half Dollar, Prince waited for the Golden Gate team to reach him. Once they arrived, Prince tied in with them, and the three retreated to the base of the wall. By the time they got to the ground, YOSAR personnel were on scene and had confirmed Klein and Wells did not survive the fall.

ANALYSIS

There are many unknowns about the accident. No one was able to see the moment the climbers began falling or the specific events leading up to it. What follows explains the findings at the scene as well as possible.

Upon reaching the anchor atop the Half Dollar, Prince found that his rope (the one Klein had trailed) had been short-fixed to two bolts. The remainder of this rope extended approximately 50 to 60 feet to a point where it ended at a number 2 Camalot clipped with a locking carabiner in the locked position. The Camalot was not placed at a significant ledge and was judged by investigators to be a temporary placement.

According to Prince, this had not been part of the team's plan; at every other belay, Klein had stayed connected to Prince's rope. Leaving Prince's rope at the cam suggests that Klein may have needed to move higher on the wall than Prince's rope would reach (although he would have needed to retreat to Prince's line at some point to retrieve it) or that he had needed to move back down the wall and had decided to leave Prince's line at his high point. It is also possible that Wells and Klein met at the top of pitch eight (atop the Half Dollar) and then Wells may have carried Prince's rope to fix at the location of the number 2 Camalot.

Wells was likely combining pitches nine and ten into a single pitch, thus avoiding the need to build a gear anchor at the top of pitch nine. Doing this would have meant that Klein would not have had enough rope to stay at the two-bolt anchor and belay at the top of the Half Dollar. However, it was determined by investigators that a 60-meter rope *would* reach the bolted anchor atop Mammoth Terraces from the location of the number 2 Camalot.

The rope was cleanly severed within a foot of Klein's harness. The investigation found boulders about 40 feet directly below the number 2 Camalot that showed evidence of sheath and core rope material. Approximately 40 feet above the Camalot, a block was found with rope fibers on two sides, indicating the fall may have been momentarily arrested at this location.

No protection was found placed in the rock leading to Mammoth. Because the rope cut during the fall, there is a chance that gear had been placed, failed, and was lost off the end of the rope when it cut. However, the evidence suggests this was not the case.

Three unattached cams were found at the base of El Capitan near Wells. Multiple cams were attached to Wells' right gear loops. Both gear loops on the left side of Wells' harness were broken, and investigators determined that the cams found at the base likely detached from Wells' harness during the fall. (No gear was found on the route during a follow-up patrol.) The total number of cams accounted for was consistent with the total that Prince believed the team brought for the climb. If so, the two climbers would not have had either a belay or any protection between them when they fell.

A few reporting parties stated they had seen a haul bag drop off the Shield headwall (above this area of the Salathé) just before the accident. Extensive follow-up found these claims to be untrue. (*Source: Yosemite National Park Climbing Rangers.*)

Editor's note: The mysterious and unplanned number 2 cam placement suggests that one of the climbers may have tied off the trail rope while dealing with a contingency above or below that point. Perhaps the rope between Wells and Klein got stuck or a piece of gear was dropped. It's possible that one climber fell while attempting to solve this unknown problem and then his fall pulled off the other. The full story will never be known.

LEADER FALL WHILE AIDING | Inexperience, Back-cleaning
Yosemite Valley, Washington Column

On June 30, a climber fell from the Kor Roof (fourth pitch) on the South Face Route (V 5.8 C1) of Washington Column. The reporting party stated that the climber was now on Dinner Ledge and had an altered mental state after sustaining head injuries.

While preparing for a possible helicopter evacuation, a paramedic ranger quickly ascended fixed lines put in place by other teams on Dinner Ledge. Upon reaching the scene and doing an assessment, the ranger determined that the patient (male, mid-20s) was alert and oriented, and was stable enough to rappel the fixed lines with the park ranger and the rest of his team.

ANALYSIS
A later interview with the injured climber found that he had been leading the Kor Roof and back-cleaning extensively to "make things easier for his follower," at the recommendation of other parties on Dinner Ledge. However, he also stated that he

and his partner were not experienced in doing lower-outs off fixed pieces, which would have been necessary for the second climber to follow the pitch. The leader was approximately 15 to 20 feet up and right of his last piece of protection (a bolt with a long runner) when he lost his balance, and the quickdraw he was using to clip in direct to his placements (instead of daisy chains) unexpectedly unclipped or was never clipped in the first place. The climber fell almost to Dinner Ledge.

The climber said that while he had done multiple climbs in Yosemite in the past year, this was his first big wall and he felt he was using techniques that were above his skill level in that terrain. He walked away from a huge fall with minimal injuries only because of his helmet. Without this protection, the outcome might have been catastrophic. (*Source: Yosemite National Park Climbing Rangers.*)

FALL ON SNOW | Inexperience, Inadequate equipment
Sierra Nevada, Mt. Whitney

On the morning of June 10, Inyo County Search and Rescue was notified of an accident involving three climbers above Trail Camp on Mt. Whitney. At approximately 7 a.m., climber 1 (female, age unknown) slipped while ascending "The Chute," a snowfield often used as a shortcut in early season when the main route is under snow. The Chute gains about 1,200 feet, rejoining the main trail around 13,600 feet. At the time of the accident, the snow surface was likely hard or icy.

Climber 1 was ascending the snowfield, reportedly without crampons or an ice axe, when she lost her balance and began sliding. She was unable to self-arrest and tumbled down the slope, colliding with climber 2 (female, age unknown) and then climber 3 (male, age unknown), who reportedly reached out to try to stop the falling climbers and sustained a spinal injury in the ensuing collision. Climbers 1 and 2 came to a stop approximately 150 feet apart and on 30° terrain after falling almost 500 feet in elevation.

Climbers 1 and 2 suffered a number of injuries, including major head and facial trauma and pelvic and spine injuries. Other climbers, whose aid was essential to the operation, stabilized the patients' positions, preventing them from sliding farther down the slope. A California Highway Patrol helicopter ferried members of the Inyo SAR team to the accident site, where they treated Climbers 1 and 2 and packaged them for transport and hoist evacuation. Despite his injury, Climber 3 was able to hike out on his own. (*Source: Inyo County SAR.*)

ANALYSIS
Given the relatively moderate pitch of the snowfield, it seems probable the accident could have been prevented with proper equipment and experience. Climbers attempting Mt. Whitney in early season conditions should be prepared with crampons, ice axe, and helmet, should be trained and confident in self-arrest and other mountaineering techniques, and should not ascend directly below other climbers.

As an additional note, climbers should not attempt to stop an uncontrolled high-speed fall of another climber on icy terrain, but rather move out of the fall path if possible and then downclimb to assist any injured climbers. (*Sources: Inyo County SAR and the Editors.*)

TRAPPED BY TALUS BOULDER
Sierra Nevada, Mt. Conness

On July 29, after climbing North Peak, Kimberly Luba and I descended to the basin below Mt. Conness. While resting by a small alpine lake, we heard cries for help. We headed up the talus field under the north ridge of Conness, following the screams. Before long I located a 21-year-old male, Adrien Costa, who had been making a solo attempt on a direct line up to the north ridge. At around 11,400 feet, a large piece of unstable talus had shifted and fallen onto his leg, just above the knee, trapping him. The incident occurred at approximately 12:45 p.m. It was now 1 p.m.

Primary assessment revealed a crushing injury to the right leg caused by the granite block, which was roughly 5x5x1 feet in size and weighed about two tons. There was no sensation or mobility below the injury but slow capillary refill in the calf. The femur, knee, and lower leg all had significant deformity. The patient had significant bleeding from the site of the injury that appeared to be arterial. He was alert and oriented with stable vitals and but severe pain. I applied an improvised tourniquet with a small piece of rope and a carabiner at 1:05 p.m. and activated my SPOT device. (It was later determined the device never sent the message despite it reporting a successful transmission.) We waved a red jacket and used a whistle to signal another party on Mt. Conness, who called for help on their cell phone.

Preparing to move a two-ton talus block from a trapped climber (center, red jacket) below Mt. Conness. *Sam England*

We provided fluids to Adrien, but he had no appetite for food. The tourniquet successfully stopped the bleeding, and his vitals and level of consciousness were stable. At 4 p.m., unsure of whether help was coming, I left Kimberly with Adrien and began hiking toward the car, planning to call 911 and then return to the accident site with bivy gear. After 20 minutes, I intercepted a Mono County Sheriff's Department SAR team and escorted them to the site, where they took over the scene at roughly 4:45 p.m.

The SAR team called the National Guard for a helicopter extraction. Meanwhile, they rigged a 9:1 ratchet system to prepare to move the boulder, as well as other systems to stabilize the stone once it was moved. A Blackhawk helicopter arrived and lowered a flight paramedic, who took over medical intervention. Once the helicopter had burned enough fuel to accommodate the weight of the patient, the boulder was moved off Adrien, six hours after he became trapped. He was packaged into a litter and carried over the talus and onto the glacier, where he and the medic were winched into the helicopter and flown out. Adrien's leg was later amputated above the knee.

ANALYSIS

I am unaware of the events leading up to the accident, as we arrived shortly after it happened. Obviously, care should be taken when crossing loose talus. Although

Adrien was not on the traditional route to the north ridge of Conness, I believe he intended to take the line he followed. There are risks in climbing alone. [*Editor's note: Indeed, the patient was very fortunate there were people nearby who could reach him quickly and were able to control his bleeding.*] (Source: Sam England.)

FALL ON ROCK | Downclimbing Fourth-Class Terrain
Sierra Nevada, Palisades, Thunderbolt Peak

At approximately 4:30 p.m. on August 26, two climbers were descending loose 4th-class terrain in the North Couloir of Thunderbolt Peak when a male climber (31) took a tumbling fall of approximately 300 feet, suffering major trauma. This climber had belayed his partner (female, 38) down this passage and was downclimbing to her when he fell. He ended up in a low-angled scree- and talus-covered area at 13,400 feet. The party had a personal locator beacon (PLB), which was activated immediately.

An air search located a headlamp high on Thunderbolt Peak that evening, but due to waning daylight and high altitude, no rescue was possible at that time. On the morning of August 27, the Inyo County Sheriff's Office initiated a helicopter response. The crew reported strong and turbulent winds near the climbers' location that prevented them from approaching the party or landing below their position. After picking up an Inyo County Search and Rescue team member, the helicopter crew found that westerly updrafts near the ridge crest would permit them to lower the Inyo SAR member onto the ridge at 13,800 feet. (This is likely one of the highest-elevation helicopter lowers ever performed in California.) Over the next five hours, four additional rescuers and equipment were lowered to the ridge.

The Inyo SAR team members descended to the climbers' location, initiated care, and packaged the injured climber in a full-body vacuum splint and Sked stretcher for extraction. The patient was lowered approximately 250 feet down low-angle rock, snow, and ice to a point where an Army National Guard CH-47 Chinook helicopter could hoist and transport him to medical care. The climber's injuries included several unstable cervical vertebrae fractures, other fractures throughout his body, and a pneumothorax. He lost consciousness for a significant period of time but was verbally responsive by the time the Inyo SAR team arrived.

Climber's smashed helmet after a long tumble in the North Couloir of Thunderbolt Peak. *Inyo SAR*

SAR team members and the partner descended to the bottom of the couloir and bivouacked nearby. They were evacuated by helicopter the next day.

ANALYSIS
The cause of the actual fall is unknown. The injured climber had belayed his partner down the 4th-class terrain, but it is unknown whether she placed protection for him or was belaying him as he downclimbed after her. The terrain where the accident occurred, like many couloirs in the High Sierra, has abundant loose rock and scarce opportunities for reliable protection or belay anchors. The party's method of descent

was typical for such terrain, which generally must be treated as "no falls" territory, requiring constant attention. [See "Know the Ropes: Safer 4th Class" in ANAC 2018.]

Even though the party carried a PLB, enabling a quicker response, approximately 27 hours elapsed between the time of the accident and evacuation. Fortunately, the party was well equipped for an unplanned overnight stay. Additionally, and under very challenging circumstances, the partner was able to maneuver the patient to a stable position and keep him warm while awaiting rescue, which improved his chances of survival and recovery. (*Source: Inyo County SAR.*)

LOWERING ERROR | Miscommunication
Bishop, Pine Creek Canyon, Gateway Slabs

On October 20, at approximately 2 p.m., an experienced climber (male, 36) took a long, tumbling ground fall on Vanadium Miner's Daughter (5.9) at the Gateway Slabs, outside of Pratt's Crack Canyon. This single-pitch climb on a low-angle slab was the party's third route of the day. Prior to reaching the anchor, the climber asked the belayer (male, 35) if he wanted to do the route. The belayer replied that he would clean it on top-rope. The climber continued to the anchor, clipped in, and yelled "take." At some point, the belayer thought he had heard the climber say "off belay" and took the climber off. When the climber leaned back after yelling "take," he fell to the ground.

The climber suffered numerous fractures and internal injuries. Inyo County SAR and local fire/EMS units transported the climber to the hospital. He was expected to fully recover from his injuries. (*Source: Inyo County SAR.*)

ANALYSIS
This incident reinforces the importance of clear communication between a climber and belayer. Communicating the plan for descending from the anchor *before* beginning the route is a must, especially in situations when the anchor is out of sight or when communication may be difficult (e.g. long pitches, crowded crags, wind or road noise). If the belayer hears "off belay" (or anytime the belayer hears an unexpected instruction), it is critical to confirm this with the climber. Finally, a climber should always confirm the belayer is ready to lower and then test-weight the lowering system *before* unclipping from the anchor. (*Sources: Inyo County SAR and the Editors.*)

LEADER FALL ON ROCK | Loose Rock, Inadequate Protection
Sierra National Forest, Windy Cliff

I try to climb a first ascent on my birthday, October 20, every year, and this time my friends Vitaliy and Adam and I had selected the south face of Windy Cliff. It lies on the north side of the South Fork of the Kings River, just outside of Kings Canyon National Park. The rock is marble, which can have notoriously bad sections.

After a search for the best looking rock on the cliff, Vitaliy took the first pitch, and Adam and I followed up to a small stance. I started hesitantly up the second pitch, testing the rock carefully before every move. When I reached a short bulge, I placed a bolt above the lip, as there was no adequate protection nearby. I placed a number 3 Camalot about four feet above the bolt, and the rock quality improved noticeably.

There was a nice ledge ahead, with a number 3 size crack above it, so I reached down and back-cleaned the Camalot below my feet before continuing.

There were a couple of thin moves before the ledge. After knocking on one grapefruit-size hold, I could tell it wasn't super solid, but the climbing was less than vertical so I thought it would stay in place if I didn't pull out on it. However, as I began to transfer my weight, the hold came loose. My reflex was to push the rock back into position to keep it from hitting my partners or the rope. This worked, but I came off and began sliding down the rock with my hands extended straight up and my toes pointing straight down. After falling about 15 feet, I hit a small ledge about the size of a license plate. I bounced off this ledge and fell six feet more before the rope caught me.

Only the balls of my feet had hit the small stance, which forced my toes toward my shins. The tendon of my calf muscle (flexor hallucis longus) in both legs tightened until it fractured the inside of my calcaneous in my left foot and shattered the calcaneous in my right foot. My feet quickly swelled and I had to remove my shoes. Vitaliy and Adam lowered me to their stance, then down to the ground with our other rope.

Vitaliy is an emergency department nurse, and Adam is a physical therapist, and they made the wise suggestion that we use my emergency beacon to call for help. However, I was not comfortable with asking rescuers to try to reach me in this windy canyon without a life-threatening injury, so I put tape on my hands and started scooting down the gully toward the river. Adam and Vitaliy carried all the gear, setting rappels on the sections that were too steep to scoot. They carried me across the Kings River, and I crawled the remaining stretch up to the road.

ANALYSIS

I made a beginner mistake: I knew there was a chance of loose rock, and yet I was moving quickly to make up for lost time. If I had not back-cleaned the cam (or had brought more protection), I would have stopped falling above the impact point. I am generally very careful to protect routes to avoid hitting the ground or ledges, but was not as careful as I should have been here. A tiny ledge can have the same effect as a large ledge if you hit it wrong. (*Source: Daniel Jeffcoach.*)

COLORADO

LOWERING ERROR | No Stopper Knot
Clear Creek Canyon, Creekside

On April 28, three buddies and I set out to climb Playin' Hooky, a three- or four-pitch bolted 5.8. By the time we made it to the crag, there were two other parties waiting to get on the same route. We checked the book and decided to get on the route next door: Furlough Day, reported to be a 125-foot 5.9. I loaded up on quickdraws and set off.

The belay platform was a shelf of rock about 20 feet above Clear Creek. The route traversed climber's left for about 20 feet to the first bolt. After clipping this bolt I was feeling relieved, because a fall before then would have taken me straight into the river.

I climbed the route with one fall. On the way down, my belay partner, who has more climbing experience than me, lowered me at a good pace. He stopped me at the third bolt to unclip the rope, then lowered me to the second bolt to do the same. (This was in hope that the rope would stay clipped to the first bolt when we pulled it, so the next leader would not have to make the same unprotected traverse.) I remember unclipping the rope from that second bolt and then free-falling.

I saw my belay partner reaching for the falling rope, and I heard and felt a thump as I hit the belay deck. Seconds after that, I fell into the icy river below. I shot up out of the water, stunned but alive. I felt no pain at that moment, just utter disbelief. I had cuts and scrapes on my body, and blood was soaking my pants.

Once my belay partner got down to me, he patched up my elbows, which both had some nice splits in them. After I'd sat on the bank for about 10 minutes, the pain started to set in. I had a feeling that my left shoulder or wrist, and maybe my ribs, were broken. However, I determined that I did not need a rescue. I limped about a quarter of a mile to the car, and we drove to the closest urgent care center.

I ended up with a collapsed lung, two broken ribs, two stitches in my elbow, and contusions in my right elbow and right buttock. I was transferred to a hospital and admitted for the collapsed lung.

The Creekside area, showing the approximate line of Furlough Day (5.9). (The first pitch finishes just above the top of the photo.) When a climber was lowered off the end of his 70-meter rope, he fell past the belay ledge and into Clear Creek below. The route Black Gold, described in a report on the next page, starts just to the left. *Dougald MacDonald*

ANALYSIS

We were climbing on a 70-meter rope, which is considered adequate for lowering from the first-pitch anchors of Furlough Day. [*Editor's note: Although this pitch is longer than one half of a 70-meter rope, it is possible to lower to the belay ledge with a 70m with care. One of the two current guidebooks to this area and Mountain Project stress the length of the pitch and the importance of tying a stopper knot at the belayer's end of the rope. It's also important to note that rope lengths vary, generally shrinking with use and age, and not all "70s" are the same.*] As I was lowering, my belay partner did not notice the rope had almost run out even though I still needed to descend another 20 feet. The end of the rope zipped through the belay device, which led to my fall. We both shared responsibility for the mistakes that were made. We should have tied a stopper knot in the rope and taken more time with this exposed descent. I blame this a lot on myself and my anxious tendencies to go, go, go. (*Source: Patrick Stefanik.*)

Editor's note: Patrick Stefanik was interviewed about this incident for episode 32 of the Sharp End podcast.

STRANDED | Stuck Rappel Ropes
Clear Creek Canyon, Creekside

On both August 18 and October 3, the Alpine Rescue Team responded to the east end of the Creekside wall to assist stranded climbers. The climbers had started up the neighboring multi-pitch sport routes Playin' Hooky (5.8) and Black Gold (5.7), and in each case they had ended up at the final belay anchor for Black Gold. In both instances, the climbers rappelled directly from bolts set at least 10 feet back from the edge of the cliff. Each used a single 70-meter rope to rappel, barely reached the roomy ledge and belay anchors below the last pitch of Black Gold. Because of excessive friction, the climbers could not pull down their ropes, and they ended up calling 911. One pair made their call well after sundown, resulting in a cold, dark wait. Rescuers hiked up the walk-off trail, and two rescuers rappelled from the Playin' Hooky anchors to the stranded climbers, then helped them down the next three rappels.

ANALYSIS

While the three-bolt anchor atop Black Gold was convenient for topping out, this was never intended to be a rappel anchor. Rather, the bolts were placed as the anchor for a slackline across the adjacent gully long before the climbing route existed. Besides being well back from the edge of the cliff, the bolts also are slightly below the edge, causing rappel ropes to bend more than 90° and resulting in significant friction.

After word got out about the stranded August climbers, Black Gold's first ascensionist added temporary warning tags to the bolts, one saying "NO RAPPEL HERE" and the other "RAPPEL PLAYIN HOOKY," with an arrow pointing to the climber's left. (The Playin' Hooky top anchor is about 25 feet to the left.) When asked why they ignored these tags, one of the October climbers replied, "We thought the tag meant not to use that specific bolt." [*User-friendly rappel anchors now are in place for this route.*] In addition to the possibility of rappelling the neighboring line, there is a walk-off from the top that follows a climbers' trail north and around the top of the obvious gully, then down the next gully to the east.

Situational awareness is an acquired skill, gained through experience, but the process can be accelerated by climbing with skilled instructors and experienced mentors. With a little extra knowledge and gear, the climbers likely would have been able to recognize the problems with this anchor, identify a rope that might get stuck (conducting a pull test once over the edge), or deal with a stuck rope (carrying prusiks to ascend back up). In addition, carrying an extra layer, especially in spring and fall, can add some comfort when things do not go according to plan. (*Sources: Dale Atkins and Curt Honcharik, Alpine Rescue Team.*)

LEADER FALL ON ROCK | Off-Route
Eldorado Canyon, Redgarden Wall

On October 20, Alex Kissinger (28) and I (27) started up the Yellow Spur (six pitches, 5.9+). At around 4 p.m. we reached the top of the fourth pitch, where the belay stance is a small, exposed ledge no bigger than a small nightstand table. There are two variations for the fifth pitch, according to the guidebook and Mountain Project: You can go straight up a piton/bolt ladder to a headwall leading into the next pitch (5.9+/10a)

ESSENTIALS

TRAUMATIC STRESS INJURIES
IMMEDIATE AND LONG-TERM AID

By Laura McGladrey

It's early season on El Cap. A climber looks up to see his partner peel off the rock and fly past him. When the climber rappels down, his fallen partner is barely responsive. Yosemite Search and Rescue arrives soon and evacuates the fallen climber. They lead the uninjured climber to the ground. The partner survives the fall and recovers from the injuries, returning to climbing. However, two years later, the "uninjured" climber still can't bring himself to get back out on the rock. In fact, he's quietly sold off his gear and has bought a mountain bike.

STRESS INJURY FORMATION

There is growing recognition of traumatic stress injuries in climbers, mountaineers, and rescuers who experience overwhelming events such as the death of a climbing partner or a near miss in an avalanche. When a climber watches a partner rappel off the end of the rope, their own life is forever changed.

Critical incidents and near misses share similar characteristics that overwhelm one's response system, establish a connection to the injured person, or create a profound sense of helplessness. While attention tends to focus on the physically injured in an accident, the partner who witnessed the event may struggle to return to the sport, long after the injured person has made a physical recovery.

The physiological response to stress is both normal and expected, and helps one cope with a threat. Stress injuries are formed when the brain's limbic system, which is responsible for our survival, is overwhelmed or feels out of control. This can take place even after the stimulus has passed, inducing a state of constant arousal that leads to a significant impact on function and relationships, as well as long-term physical and mental health.

Organizations such as the American Alpine Club, Outward Bound, NOLS Wilderness Medicine, and the Mountain Rescue Association (MRA) are now discussing stress injuries as a wilderness injury type. NOLS Wilderness Medicine even teaches stress injury alongside head, chest, and spine injuries, emphasizing this as an injury type with significant impact to the wilderness rescuer.

ASSESSMENT

Social withdrawal, substance abuse, hyper-vigilance, flashbacks, and anxiety are known to be associated with one type of stress injury, commonly referred to as "post-traumatic stress disorder" (PTSD). However, the more subtle or earlier signs of stress injury formation are rarely discussed. Choosing to stop participating in the activities we once loved, a short temper, loss of confidence, or avoidance of assisting with a rescue are among the changes associated with exposure to traumatic events.

Various outdoor and rescue organizations are now using a tool called the Stress Continuum to better assist their members in understanding stress injuries. The

PSYCHOLOGICAL FIRST AID (PFA)
SAFETY
• Stabilize the scene
• Use language of safety ("Now that you are safe...")
• Protect partner(s) from more stress
CALM
• Demonstrate calm, empathetic listening
• Alleviate connected anxiety ("Your partner is safe, now let's take care of you")
ENGAGEMENT
• Involve partners in problem solving
• Assign a job
CONNECTION
• Build on-scene relationship
• Use partner and rescuer names
• Connect partners with family, friends, loved ones, pets ASAP
HOPE
• Keep positive ("We got this")
• Offer chronological steps of rescue
• Be future oriented

Stress Continuum was first used by the U.S. Marine Corps and has been adapted for use by climbing organizations and individuals to assess how climbers will fare after witnessing overwhelming events. [A *sample continuum chart can be seen with this story at publications.americanalpineclub.org.*] People experiencing feelings in the middle of the continuum, such as cynicism, lack of interest, and a short temper, may be reacting to a critical incident and will be less likely to return to vibrant climbing experiences. The goal of the model is earlier recognition of injury formation, allowing for early mitigation rather than waiting for the development of PTSD.

TREATMENT

Psychological first aid (PFA) is now included in many wilderness medicine curricula. PFA recognizes the need to decrease arousal immediately following significant events (*see chart on this page*). It is a simple, pragmatic intervention designed to enhance the components of resiliency and mitigate the initial stress response: re-creating a sense of **safety**, communicating a sense of **calm**, encouraging social support and building **connection**, re-establishing a sense of **self-efficacy**, and creating **hope** for realistic and accurate steps ahead.

Treatment of a stress injury that develops after an incident begins with awareness and recognition. Use of the Stress Continuum allows for an early warning system in high-exposure roles, such as helicopter rescue. Many organizations now invest in practices known to mitigate stress states, such as connection, engagement, post-incident support, and support of a vibrant life outside of climbing. The central goal is to build internal capacity to sustain and integrate overwhelming events as they occur.

For individual climbers, personality changes, decreased desire or fear when climbing, difficulty concentrating, isolation, or reckless climbing can all be indicators that one was impacted and would benefit from more support. Support in this setting may include recognizing there has been a change, sharing what's happening with people who "get it," or working with a trauma therapist who "speaks climber." This injury type can absolutely be supported when recognized.

Laura McGladrey is a nurse practitioner in Colorado, as well as a NOLS instructor and stress and adversity advisor to search and rescue and ski patrol teams. She was interviewed about stress injury and psychological first aid for episode 34 of the Sharp End podcast. Resources related to stress injury can be found at responderalliance.com, samhsa.gov, and ptsd.va.gov. In addition, the AAC is developing a program called the Climbing Grief Fund that aims to help climbers who have experienced traumatic episodes or loss. Information and updates are at americanalpineclub.org/climbing-grief-fund.

or go up to the first piton then move out left to the more moderate but exposed "Robbins Traverse" (5.7+ PG-13), or so I had understood the options. [*Editor's note: The guidebook actually says to climb to the first* bolt *before starting the Robbins Traverse.*]

I started leading the fifth pitch, climbing an arête for 10 to 15 feet, and clipped the first piton I saw. I had read that if taking the traverse variation it's best to extend the runner on the first piton to reduce rope drag. I clipped the piton with a double-length sling, then backed up the piton with a number 1 Metolius Ultralight Master Cam a foot to the left in a horizontal crack. I double extended the cam as well to reduce any form of rope drag. I then moved left into the exposed traverse.

Immediately, the climbing was more insecure than anything we had done on the lower pitches (up to 5.9+). I slowly moved up and left, then made three or four moves to advance five vertical feet. I scanned for protection placements, but there were none. I started to feel fatigued, saw what looked like a shallow, chalk-dusted horn up to my right, just beyond a static reach, and committed to throwing for it. I missed.

What I remember next is the feeling of free fall, air quickly filling the top of my chest, then a second later I opened my eyes and was hanging next to Alex, slightly below the belay ledge. I saw blood on the wall beneath me and on my hands. I had fallen 30 to 40 feet and was unconscious for three minutes. Alex tells me that I fell on him, hit the small belay stance, then slammed against a wall before I was arrested by the rope. The back of my helmet was cracked. According to Alex, once my fall was arrested, I started convulsing for around 30 seconds, then my body went limp as I hung from my harness 10 feet below him.

Alex extended his anchor tether and managed to pull me up next to him and clip me to the anchor. He used his shirt to apply pressure on my head and reduce the bleeding, and he called 911 and yelled to other climbers at the base of the wall to do the same. At around 6:30 p.m., Rocky Mountain Rescue Group rappelled in and began to help us down. We reached the ground at around 9:30 p.m. With assistance I was able to walk out of the canyon.

I was diagnosed with a concussion, intracranial hemorrhage, a large laceration on the back left side of my head, which required 14 staples to mend, and a puncture wound in my left calf. I recovered fully.

ANALYSIS

Before any route, especially a traditional multi-pitch route, no matter how classic or well-traveled, always do as much research as possible to prevent getting off route. I now know that I moved left for the traverse way too early. This lack of due diligence was the cause of my accident. I am very grateful for my partner's quick reaction and for keeping me alive, and to the volunteers of Rocky Mountain Rescue Group for getting me down. I am also glad I was wearing a helmet, which undoubtedly saved me from a more serious head injury or potential death. (*Source: David Rozul.*)

Editor's note: It's easy to fall into the trap of forcing off-route climbing to match a guidebook description, and therefore it's important to stay alert for signs you've wandered off the line. In this case, the lack of chalk, lack of protection, and unexpected difficulties each could have been red flags on such a well-traveled, reasonably protected climb. When the "off route" signs start flashing, it's better to downclimb to a stance, regroup, and study the alternatives than to go for it and hope for the best.

CONNECTICUT

LEAD FALL ONTO LEDGE | Protection Pulled Out
Ragged Mountain, Main Cliff

On November 10, in very cold temperatures, Sam Warren (20) and his partner were rock climbing at Main Cliff on Ragged Mountain. Sam, a 5.10 sport climber and beginner trad climber, was attempting to lead Tower Crack (5.7), an offwidth crack in an inside corner. When first climbed in 1935 by Fritz Wiessner, Tower Crack was among the hardest rock climbs in the country. Sam was confident, having previously followed Tower Crack and having led crack climbs of similar difficulty.

Sam approached the crack by climbing up Wiessner's Slab for about 70 feet to the large horizontal ledge below the upper offwidth corner. He placed a large cam (size unknown) at the bottom of the corner and a number 0.3 Black Diamond Camalot in a crack in a side wall higher up. While attempting to move up the climb, he fell twice onto the small cam without injury. On his third attempt at the crux, he fell again and pulled out the 0.3, hitting a ledge and spraining his left ankle. He and his partner were able to rappel to the ground and hike out. Fortunately, his injuries were minor and he recovered in a few weeks. (*Source: Sam Warren.*)

ANALYSIS
The piece protecting the crux and keeping the climber from hitting the ledge had shifted and was no longer well positioned. It may have shifted from the prior falls, the climber bumping the piece as he moved past it in bulky wintertime clothing, or due to the use of a short quickdraw. Anytime you fall onto a piece, reassess its placement and ensure it is still good. Micro-cams, like the 0.3 that pulled out, have particularly small margins for error. Rope stretch may have contributed to hitting the ledge, and stretch could have been minimized by making an intermediate belay on the ledge below the crux crack. (*Sources: Sam Warren and the Editors.*)

IDAHO

FALL AND AVALANCHE | Inexperience, Climbing Alone
Lost River Range, Borah Peak

Hao Yan, 23, had come to Idaho from the East Coast to fight forest fires, and in June he decided to attempt 12,662-foot Borah Peak. Climbing solo, he started before dawn but got lost on the approach, and by the time he reached the main difficulties on the northeast ridge it was 6 p.m. A steep rock step (complicated by mixed climbing in June) bars access to the top. The climber started up this section, using a rope and some form of self-belay, but 20 to 25 feet up, his "anchor suddenly broke from the rock" and he fell to the base of the step, then continued sliding down the north side of the mountain in an avalanche triggered by his fall. He came to a stop several hundred feet down, tangled in gear and reportedly buried up to his neck in snow.

The climber attempted to continue down the mountain, but pain in his legs, neck, and back prevented him from moving far. He was able to get a signal on his mobile phone and called for help around 9:30 p.m. Custer County Search and Rescue decided to call for a helicopter team from Kalispell, Montana, to expedite the search, and at around 2 a.m. rescuers spotted the climber in a snowfield below the north face. He was flown to a hospital and treated for hypothermia and possible spinal fractures.

The north face of Borah Peak (12,662 feet), with the northeast ridge on the left skyline. The climber fell from the prominent rock step at the bottom of the steep ridge and then slid down snow below the north face. *Dan Robbins*

(*Sources: East Idaho News and other published reports, online interview with the climber.*)

ANALYSIS

Hao Yan reported having some mountaineering experience, including taking classes with Colorado Mountain School. This northeast ridge can be climbed at class 4 in ideal conditions and if the correct route is followed, but many climbers encounter 5th-class terrain. In June it would have significant snow or mixed climbing. Although it's not known exactly what caused his fall, starting the crux after 6 p.m. meant he likely was fatigued and had very little time for a safe ascent and descent. Climbing alone, he was very fortunate to have a viable cell phone signal to call for help after his tumble. (*Source: The Editors.*)

KENTUCKY

FALL FROM ANCHOR | Rappel Error
Red River Gorge, Muir Valley, Sunnyside

On April 27, Seamus Hehir (26) fell approximately 50 feet after incorrectly setting up a rappel to clean the route Suppress the Rage (5.12a) at Sunnyside wall. According to his belayer, Jake McCrary (32), Seamus hit a boulder at the base of the climb and continued falling down an embankment roughly 20 feet. McCrary called 911 while another member of their climbing party, a physician assistant, began first aid. Wolfe County Search and Rescue responded, and Hehir was airlifted to a Level I trauma center in Lexington. He sustained a broken back, a broken neck, and a head laceration. He was not wearing a helmet.

Due to the nature of the injuries, the climber has little memory of the accident or setting up the rappel. The climbers at the base of the route removed Hehir's rappel device from his harness after he fell, and McCrary said that only one line was clipped through the tube-style device. After the incident, the rope ran from the base up through the quickdraws on the route and then down to the climber on the ground, but it was not threaded through the anchors. McCrary concluded that Hehir had only clipped his device with the side of the rope that ran from the ground through the draws, then pulled the other side through the anchors during his fall. Hehir typically cleans routes by rappel and says that he regularly attaches an autoblock, but does not recall if he used an autoblock in this instance. McCrary is also unsure if he removed an autoblock following the incident.

ANALYSIS

From the accounts of the event, it seems as if only one strand of the rappel rope was threaded through the tube-style rappel device and clipped to Hehir's harness with a locking carabiner. As noted above, he may have used an autoblock backup, but autoblocks are not effective safeguards when the two strands of rappel ropes are pulling in opposite directions, as they would when a rappeller fails to clip both strands properly. (See p.105 for a similar incident in Wyoming.)

Hehir had over five years of outdoor climbing experience at the time of the incident and usually cleans gear on rappel unless the route is very steep. His recommendation is to stay attentive and present, take your time, and carefully perform safety checks before rappelling. He said he was on his feet in a comfortable stance as he prepared to rappel, and thus may not have fully weighted his rappel system before unclipping his tether from the anchors. Hehir also suspects he may have been rushing through the familiar steps, as this was the last climb of the day and the group was attending a pre-wedding event later that evening. (Sources: Seamus Hehir, Jake McCrary, and Wolfe County Search and Rescue.)

Editor's note: In the Red River Gorge, it is generally an accepted practice to lower off anchors to clean a route.

Pulling off a large block while top-roping in the Red River Gorge. Luckily, neither the climber nor belayer was seriously injured. *Patrick Miller Collection*

FALL ON ROCK | Huge Loose Block
Red River Gorge, Miller Fork, Camelot

On June 10, Jason Harbin (47) and I (45) climbed the Keeper (5.9), a relatively new (2017) sport route at Camelot. We stick-clipped the high first bolt and I led the route with no issues. Jason (12 years of climbing experience) opted to clean the route on top-rope. As Jason approached the first bolt, he pulled off an approximately four- by eight-foot block (eight to 12 inches thick).

STAY OFF WET SANDSTONE

Two reports in this edition describe climbers being injured after pulling off large sandstone flakes. In neither case was recent rain believed to be the culprit, but wet sandstone is very susceptible to breaking. In addition to potentially ruining a good climb by destroying holds, serious injury is possible from broken holds or insecure protection.

There are many variables—relative softness of the sandstone, duration and intensity of rain or snow, sun exposure, etc.—but a good rule of thumb is to stay off any sandstone climbs in the desert Southwest for 24 to 48 hours after a steady rain or snowstorm. If in doubt, scuff the soil or sand under a climb to see if there is moisture beneath the surface; if so, the rock may also still be wet and fragile.

When it comes to sandstone climbs, remember this: "Mud on your feet? Retreat!"

The block released and fell so quickly that Jason held onto it, causing him to invert and dragging him down the wall. The weight of the fall pulled me toward the wall, and the block landed about six inches away from me, shattering upon impact. Two large pieces remained on our packs and shoes. Jason was left hanging upside down about 10 feet from the ground, his back covered in a bloody rock rash but with no other injuries. (*Source: Patrick Miller.*)

ANALYSIS

We were very lucky that everyone was able to walk away from this event. If I had not been paying attention or if Jason had decided to lead the route, the consequences could have been much worse. Since Camelot is a newer crag in Miller Fork, the route had not seen a lot of traffic. It is important for developers to identify and mitigate potential hazards as they clean and bolt their routes, keeping in mind that future climbers may apply more force on holds in varying directions.

This was a pretty typical block/flake feature seen throughout the Red. Before Jason released the block, I had pulled, manteled, and stood on it, unaware of the hazard. As climbers, we need to be aware that routes, especially new ones, are prone to breakage, and we need to be vigilant about our safety. (*Source: Patrick Miller, Lindsay Auble, and the Editors.*)

SNAKEBITE
Red River Gorge, Muir Valley, Bruise Brothers

On October 6, a 25-year-old female was climbing a route at Bruise Brothers wall in Muir Valley. Approximately 15 feet up the route, she was bitten by a copperhead snake after placing her hand within a crack. Venom was received from the bite, resulting in significant pain. The climber was assisted back to the parking area and transported via ambulance to a local hospital.

ANALYSIS

Dangerous wildlife encounters are not common in the Red River Gorge. Snakebites (primarily from the copperhead) are the most prevalent wildlife encounter that results in a visit to an emergency department. The Wolfe County Search and Rescue (SAR) team responds to only one or two snakebites per year, and most incidents are unrelated to climbing.

Wolfe County SAR recommends that climbers be mindful of snakes on cool mornings in the spring and fall. Snakes are cold-blooded and seek out locations to warm their bodies, taking advantage of rocky cliff lines and boulders that retain heat. Copperheads are not typically aggressive, but will strike without warning

Native to the Southeast, the copperhead's range extends north to Massachusetts and west to Texas. Centers for Disease Control

when threatened. Climbers should avoid throwing out food scraps that draw mice and other small animals to a crag, as snakes will follow their food source. Muir Valley posts signs in areas where copperheads are known to frequent or den.

If a climber is bitten by a venomous snake, Wolfe County SAR recommends seeking immediate medical attention. Stay calm and remove any tight-fitting clothing and jewelry near the bite. Irrigate the wound with clean water as soon as possible to remove any remaining venom at or near the surface of the skin. Apply a clean dressing and, if possible, take a photo of the snake and note coloring and pattern from a safe distance. (Do not attempt to capture or kill the snake.) Walk the injured person to a vehicle, keeping the affected limb at the level of the heart, if possible. If the skin begins to turn red and swell, take a photo or mark the outer edges with a pen and note the time. This will help medical providers better estimate the degree of envenomation. (*Source: John May, Chief, Wolfe County Search and Rescue and the Editors.*)

MINNESOTA

FALL FROM TOP OF CLIFF | Inadequate Protection
Taylor's Falls

On July 9, a 23-year-old man with about two months of climbing experience was scouting for new climbs at the top of a popular crag called Taylor's Falls, one hour north of Minneapolis–Saint Paul. The climber was not wearing a harness, helmet, or any other climbing gear when he slipped and fell about 50 feet to the rocky landing below. The fall was witnessed by some girls who were canoeing on the river nearby. Their counselor hiked to the injured person's location, face down in a rocky crevice. Chisago County emergency services responded, and the person was transported via boat to an ambulance and then flown via helicopter to Regions Hospital in Saint Paul. The climber sustained fractured vertebrae, ribs, skull, and various other bones in the head and face.

ANALYSIS

Though not strictly a "climbing accident," such falls from the tops of cliffs occur nearly every year, and unfortunately they often are fatal. Slippery grass, moss, and leaves, wet or loose rock, roots, loose soil, and snow or ice can all be slipping or tripping hazards at the tops of cliffs. Whether preparing for a rappel descent, approaching the edge of a cliff to set up a top-rope, or scouting for routes, as in this case, it's best to err on the side of caution and create a temporary anchor to secure your approach to any cliff edge. (*Sources: Andrew Rzepka and the Editors.*)

STRANDED | Knee Stuck In Wide Crack
Sandstone, Robinson Park

On August 2, a 13-year-old girl was climbing with a camp group at Robinson Park in Sandstone, about an hour and a half north of Minneapolis–Saint Paul, when she got her knee stuck in a wide crack 40 feet above the ground. Climbers in her group were able to secure her from above, but were unable to free her knee. After several attempts, they called 911 at about 3:30 p.m. Authorities from Pine County Sheriff's Office, St. Louis County Rescue, and Isanti Fire Department responded. The girl's knee was quite swollen by the time the rescuers arrived. They used dish soap to lubricate the area as well as a hammer and chisel and Jaws of Life to break away the rock, and eventually freed her at around 8 p.m. She sustained minor soft-tissue injuries.

ANALYSIS

While not a common occurrence, it is quite possible to get digits or limbs stuck in cracks. Here, the climbers did the right thing by securing the stuck person to the wall in order to take weight off her knee while attempting to free her. Many first-aid kits contain packets of surgical lubricant or petroleum jelly that can make it easier to free stuck limbs. Using it quickly may make a difference—the longer the body part is stuck, the more it will swell. (*Sources: Sarah Koniewicz and the Editors.*)

NEVADA

GROUND FALL | Detached Flake
Red Rock, Moderate Mecca

At 2 p.m. on March 28, Parker Kempf (28) dislodged a large sandstone flake (approximately three cubic feet in size) at the overhanging start of Is It Soup Yet (5.10b) in the Moderate Mecca area. This resulted in a ground fall of roughly six feet, with the detached flake landing on his lower legs.

Kempf suffered an open fracture and dislocation to the left fibula, cartilage damage to the left knee, and a fractured right tibia. His partner provided immediate first aid, including applying pressure to the bleeding wound. Due to the nature of the terrain, he eventually was airlifted to a waiting ambulance to be transported to the hospital. (*Source: Parker Kempf.*)

The start of Is It Soup Yet (5.10b), showing the approximate dimensions of the flake that broke off. The circle above marks the first protection bolt on the route. *Parker Kempf Collection*

ANALYSIS

There had been no rain at Red Rocks in the previous six days. Kempf had used this same flake earlier in the day to hang a quickdraw on the first bolt of the route for another climber and noted that it "flexed" and sounded "hollow" when he knocked on it, but no worse than other Red Rock jugs, in his judgment. Kemp's fall occurred after the climber changed her mind and decided not to do the route and he repeated the first moves to attempt to remove the quickdraw. Had he used a stick-clip to remove the quickdraw, this accident would have been avoided, but he felt that bouldering this move was easy and safe enough. Quick first aid and evacuation prevented lasting damage to his legs. Kempf was wearing a helmet, and even with this relatively short fall distance, there was damage to multiple support ribs on the back portion of the helmet. (*Sources: Parker Kempf and the Editors.*)

NEW HAMPSHIRE

LEADER FALL ON ICE | Inadequate Protection, Fatigue
Crawford Notch, Mt. Willard

On February 23, a local climbing guide, age 64, took his client to Mt. Willard, a popular area for moderate, multi-pitch ice climbs. The weather was warm, and by early afternoon freezing rain was falling. At around 1 p.m., the guide short-roped his client across a talus slope to the base of Left Hand Monkey Wrench (WI3). He placed a stubby screw on the climb's initial 20-foot traverse in order to protect his client and then placed one 13cm screw about halfway up the pitch. He headed into the narrow choke at the top of the climb, where he considered placing a third screw to protect the exit but did not do so. As he topped out the climb, his tool popped and he fell: first 20 feet onto a bench below the choke, and then an additional 20 feet. The upper 13cm screw and the belayer held his fall. The impact fractured the climber's right femur just below the hip and broke his right elbow in three places.

The guide instructed his client to tie a catastrophe knot in the belay rope to prevent him from falling further. She then ascended to his position using his weight as a counterbalance. He had come to rest in a nook in the ice, and the pair was able to work the injured guide into his emergency tarp to guard against hypothermia. They called his guiding service, and members of Mountain Rescue Service (MRS) and other guides who were on adjacent climbs rushed over to help. MRS was able to build an anchor to transfer the injured guide into a litter and then lower him through the talus and down the remaining 400 feet of steep approach gully. From there he was carried to the road, arriving around 7:30 p.m.

ANALYSIS

The length and severity of the guide's fall can be attributed to not placing a screw before the final section of climbing on the pitch. The climber was more than qualified for the difficulty of the terrain and moving quickly because he was guiding. He attributes the fall to late-season tiredness and not judging his own physical state properly before heading out. These factors are common in accidents involving guides, who will often climb quickly and without adequate protection on easy, familiar terrain. Such accidents often occur late in the day when guides are mentally exhausted.

Though the Mt. Willard area is more or less a roadside crag, the steepness of the approach and its positioning—at the apex of windy Crawford Notch—means that carrying a light emergency shelter (such as the guide's tarp) is prudent. Climbers in mountainous terrain also should carry a communication device that will allow them to call for help when cell phone service is nonexistent. (*Source: Michael Wejchert, Mountain Rescue Service.*)

LONG FALL ON SNOW | Unable to Self-Arrest

Mt. Washington, Tuckerman Ravine

At about 1 p.m. on February 24, a climber took a long sliding fall while ascending near the top of Right Gully in Tuckerman Ravine. The subject slipped on very hard, icy snow and was unable to self-arrest with an ice axe. The resulting high-speed slide was halted below the gully by exposed bushes and rocks. The fall totaled approximately 300 vertical feet.

With the help of a climbing partner, the subject was able to walk down to Hermit Lake, from which U.S. Forest Service Snow Rangers transported the subject via snowmobile to Pinkham Notch. The primary injury was presumed to be bruised or fractured ribs.

ANALYSIS

The subject and witnesses to this accident unanimously were surprised the outcome was not more serious. The subject was indeed lucky to slide into a generally bushy area as opposed to the many nearby rocks that would have likely resulted in greater injuries. Further, the subject was not wearing a helmet and was very fortunate to avoid hitting the head. The party had climbed Right Gully several times before, and other than the lack of helmets they were properly equipped with mountaineering boots, crampons, and ice axes.

While firm conditions can inspire confidence for climbers traveling uphill with crampons, it can be incredibly difficult to arrest a fall once sliding with any amount of speed, even with skilled use of an ice axe. It is better to prevent falls in the first place with solid snow climbing skills and careful movement. When unexpected conditions are encountered, it may be preferable to downclimb and retreat before climbing into a more precarious situation. (*Source: Mount Washington Avalanche Center.*)

SLIDING FALL ON SKIS | Failure to Self-Arrest
Mt. Washington, Hillman's Highway

On February 25, after climbing two-thirds of the way up Hillman's Highway and not finding a ton of good snow, our group transitioned for an icy ski descent. There was a small ribbon of wind slab on the skiers' right side of the slide. My two partners sideslipped the ice to a good point of safety. I tried the wind slab, but after a few untrustworthy turns, I bailed for the more predictable icy surface. However, on my second turn, I went down and started to slide.

I have practiced self-arresting on snow with a Whippet [self-arrest pole grip] and skis on, but not on ice. I tried to self-arrest with no luck. I slid for about 200 feet before managing to slow myself down in some soft snow piled on top of a rock. Unfortunately, as I came to a stop, I fell off the side of the rock, landing on my shoulder and dislocating it. My partners and I tried to reset the joint with no luck. We slung and secured my arm, I transitioned to crampons, and we self-rescued down to Pinkham Notch. (*Source: Anonymous report to Mount Washington Avalanche Center.*)

ANALYSIS

Once momentum is gained from an unchecked fall, it is doubtful that self-arrest ski poles or even a well-deployed ice axe would work on an icy and steep surface like the one encountered in this report. Skis also complicate self-arrest, because they may hinder a person from rolling into the best position. Downclimbing, rappelling, or sideslipping icy sections will be more secure than attempting to turn. (*Sources: Mount Washington Avalanche Center and the Editors.*)

MANY AVALANCHES
Mt. Washington, Tuckerman Ravine

On April 7, seven avalanches occurred in Tuckerman Ravine. All were human triggered. At least five people were caught in one of the avalanches.

In the week leading up to April 7, there were two rain events. The first was March 29–30, delivering 0.75 inch of rain, followed by 0.32 inch of rain on April 4. Both of these were followed by hard freezes. On Friday, April 6, light snow showers began just after noon and continued through sunrise the following day. Hermit Lake recorded 16cm (6.3") of snow, while between 7 and 8 inches was estimated at the summit. When snowfall began on Friday, wind at the summit was around 30 mph from the south. Overnight, wind direction shifted to the west and speeds increased to 60–70 mph. The weather on Saturday was clearing skies, winds diminishing to around 40 mph from the west, and temperatures in the single digits on the summit and reaching into the 20s (F) at Hermit Lake. This weather pattern built a robust melt-freeze crust, over which touchy wind slab was built from the new snow.

During the morning of April 7, three avalanches were intentionally triggered by skiers. All three were ski cuts, two occurring in Lobster Claw and one on the rollover of the Little Headwall. Slab depths were up to 14 inches, and all slides occurred on a layer of softer snow immediately above the melt-freeze crust.

Other avalanches occurred in Left Gully and Chute, both of which were triggered unintentionally. We believe that no one was caught or carried by either avalanche.

Two avalanches in Hillman's Highway this day involved a number of people being caught and carried. At approximately 2 p.m., at least 40 people were climbing and skiing in Hillman's. An individual climbing uphill from the right fork into the left fork triggered the initial avalanche. This person was not carried in the slide. The crown was approximately 300 feet below the top of Hillman's, and the slide ran two-thirds of the way down. At least five people were caught and carried. USFS snow rangers responded to the incident and identified one injured skier who was transported to Pinkham Notch with a back injury that was not life-threatening. Another individual sustained a minor injury to the hand.

Fracture line of a slab avalanche in Hillman's Highway that caught at least five people. *Kurt Schleicher*

The second avalanche was triggered around 2:30 p.m., within minutes of the initial snow ranger team arriving on scene. The consensus of bystanders is that this second avalanche was triggered by the same individual who triggered the first, after topping out on the ridge and beginning to ski the hang-fire slab above the initial crown. This second avalanche was smaller and luckily did not capture any people.

ANALYSIS

Many opportunities for learning are presented by this day, which fortunately did not involve more serious injuries. First, it's an excellent reminder that avalanche conditions can develop on Mt. Washington during the normally stable spring months, which bring crowds of backcountry skiers to Tuckerman Ravine. On days with conditions like those on April 7, anyone venturing into avalanche terrain should bring a beacon, shovel, probe, and the knowledge to use them effectively.

A cardinal rule for traveling in avalanche terrain is to move one at a time through areas exposed to avalanche danger. Despite the often-heard phrase "It's just Hillman's," all of Hillman's Highway is avalanche terrain. On top of that, it's particularly confined. Had only one person at a time been exposed in Hillman's on April 7, it's likely that nobody would have been injured. On a slope as large as Hillman's, a number of people can travel on the slope before someone finds the specific location that will trigger an avalanche. In other words, tracks on a slope do not mean it's safe to ski or climb.

Finally, we should touch on ski cutting. The process of intentionally skiing a specific part of a slope likely to trigger an avalanche, with speed, from one safe zone to another, is an advanced practice and is only appropriate under certain conditions. It is only wise when you possess a high degree of certainty about what the ski cut will produce *and* the consequences if you're wrong. In particular, ski cutting is inappropriate when an avalanche may initiate above you. On April 7, the individual ski cutting on Lobster Claw and Little Headwall was a professional skier who had high certainty both in terms of anticipated result and the consequences for being wrong, and avalanches above were nearly impossible. Further, other people were not in the potential avalanche run-out zones. (*Source: Mount Washington Avalanche Center.*)

NEW MEXICO

ROCKFALL ON RAPPEL | Darkness, Haste
Organ Mountains, Pyramid of the South Rabbit Ear

Rappelling the second pitch of the route King Slut (5.11) in the Organ Mountains is an absolute nightmare. In November, I (male, 34) was rappelling on a single 70-meter, 7.8mm half rope with a second rope on my back. Before I began navigating down a 100-foot vertical cactus garden, I tied an autoblock and knots in the end of my rope, because objective hazards were apparent and abundant. With the sun setting, I was trying to move fast and link rappels, skipping the anchor atop the first pitch, but as I rappelled over an overhang, I realized the rope ends were dangling 10 feet above the ledge where the climb had begun. This ledge sits above a 150-foot approach slab, so I couldn't risk downclimbing the remaining 10 feet to the ledge—a fall would likely be fatal.

I decided to ascend the ropes by simply pulling up on the rope strands and pulling the slack through my ATC. After one such attempt, the rotten lip of the overhang, over which the ropes were running, broke off and hit my left hand (my brake hand). I estimate the rotten mass of granite that crashed against me weighed 50 to 60 pounds, falling about five feet before hitting me. I immediately realized that my thumb was shattered, but I wasn't sure if other bones were broken. I never lost control of the ropes with my brake hand. If I had, the autoblock should have prevented a fatal ground fall.

With blood pouring out of my smashed thumb, and the autoblock already tied, I quickly set a cam in an adjacent rotten crack, clipped into it, set a fist jam with my non-broken hand, got my feet on a positive stance, and removed the ropes from my ATC. I yelled up to my partner, Dan Carter (male, 36), that I had shattered my thumb and could not make it to the ledge. He quickly rappelled down to the anchor I had skipped, threaded the ropes, and rappelled past me to the ledge. I put myself back on rappel and descended to the base of the climb. Ultimately, we were able to self-rescue, and I drove myself to an emergency room in Las Cruces.

The Rabbit Ears formation in the Organ Mountains, showing the approximate location of an unusual rappelling accident in November. *Brandon Gottung Collection*

ANALYSIS

There were a few factors that contributed to this accident. The most significant element was that it was getting dark, which made it difficult to assess the rock quality at the lip of the overhang. The pending darkness also motivated me to move faster than would be prudent in such conditions. Since I was so close to the bottom of the climb, I didn't take the time to pull out my headlamp. The second contributing factor was my increasing frustration with the horrible rappels, due to the cactus, scrub oak, and loose rock.

Luckily, I did tie an autoblock for this rappel. Even though I never let go of the ropes after I got hit, the autoblock allowed me to quickly find a stance and set an intermediate anchor. Ultimately, there is no valid reason not to tie an autoblock. (*Source: Brandon Gottung.*)

Editor's note: The old saying "slow is smooth, smooth is fast" applies here. Frustration with the conditions led to haste, which led to the decisions to link two rappels and to forego a headlamp.

NEW YORK

LEADER FALL ON ICE | Inadequate protection, Poor Position
Adirondacks, Pitchoff Mountain, North Face

On December 27, at approximately 9 a.m., my brother Don Heinz (51) and I (46) were climbing Arm and Hammer (WI3+) with two friends. It was a cold day (10° F), but there had been a recent stretch of warm weather and rain. We'd talked about canceling the trip, given the recent weather, but decided to climb anyway.

Don led the climb and headed up a 70-foot section of 50° ice to the crux, a 15-foot vertical section. He placed several screws on the low-angle start and placed another at the base of the crux before continuing up toward what he thought was solid ice. The ice sounded hollow, so he continued to climb, looking for better ice and planning to rest in a large slot at the top of the crux section. This slot was eight to ten feet tall and had been melted by rainwater. I had noted to myself that the ice looked bad in that spot but didn't mention it to my brother.

My belay was in a blind spot, so I couldn't see him climb into that area, but as he entered the V-shaped slot, he found more bad ice and continued up and left without placing another screw. Near the top of the vertical stretch, Don's left axe blew from the ice. He fell and hit the low-angle section of ice below, then continued to slide before coming to a stop hanging upside down from a screw.

No one saw him land, but his injuries suggest he impacted the ice on his left hip and back, then hit his head. He was unresponsive despite my screams from the belay. He regained consciousness after five minutes but was initially only able to make guttural noises, and I worried that he might be choking on blood. An AMGA-certified rock guide who was descending the neighboring route at the time of the accident traversed over to our route to help Don off the wall. At this point, Don was conscious but visibly confused and unstable. I lowered Don to the ground as the guide descended with him.

At the base, Don could not remember anything. He complained of pain in his left hip/back and his right shoulder. He had a puncture wound in his left side caused by an ice screw racked on his harness. We sheltered him with our puffy jackets, placed a backpack underneath him, and wrapped him in an emergency blanket provided by the guide. A member of our party called 911 and contacted the Adirondacks forest rangers. They arrived within 90 minutes of the fall, packaged Don in a litter, and lowered him down the steep hill to a point where he could be transferred to an ambulance. A helicopter then transported him to a trauma unit in Albany. His most serious injuries included a puncture wound and chip in his left hip where the tooth of the screw penetrated to the bone, three vertebrae fractures, three broken ribs on the right side, and a fracture of his right scapula. His memory returned in 24 hours, and he remained in the hospital for two days.

ANALYSIS
Between the recent weather and the obvious signs of melting, there were reasons to be concerned about the condition of the ice. A quick conversation regarding the poor ice in the slot might have alerted Don to stay away from it. A belay that provided line-of-sight to Don as he climbed also could have prevented the accident, as I would have had the opportunity to warn Don about the ice in that area.

As Don climbed the crux, he passed opportunities to place higher protection in the vertical ice section. A screw there may have prevented him from hitting the low-angle ice below the crux. Given the condition of the ice, Don should have downclimbed instead of continuing to run it out above a ledge. Don's recollection is that the last screw was eight to ten feet below him and several feet to the left when he fell, which would have resulted in a long fall even with a tight belay. After the accident, we were slow to call 911, as we were somewhat in shock.

Despite the accident, there was a lot we did right. Don's helmet clearly saved him from a very serious head injury, and the highest screw he placed saved him from a much more severe fall. Once Don was on the ground, our efforts to keep him warm were successful and prevented the situation from deteriorating further, given the cold weather. We were very fortunate to have the immediate assistance of a guide and the rangers. (*Source: Joe Heinz.*)

NEAR MISS | Unclipped from Anchor
Shawangunks, Trapps

On October 10, three climbers finished the second (last) pitch of Baby (5.6). The leader (male, 31) was using a half-rope system, with each follower tied to an end of each half rope. The leader arrived at the bolted rappel station, clove-hitched himself to the ring anchors using the half ropes and two carabiners, and built a master point by tying an overhand onto the two strands of rope. This was different from his normal routine, which used a cordelette for a belay anchor while securing himself using a personal anchor system.

Once the rest of the party arrived, they clipped themselves to the anchor with their personal tethers. As the leader began dismantling the anchor to set up the rappel, he suddenly realized he was unattached to the anchor in any way. Luckily, the team was standing on a small ledge, so the issue was corrected and the party descended safely. (*Source: Anonymous report from the leader.*)

ANALYSIS

The leader's analysis of the incident: "This happened because I deviated from my usual pattern of climbing and untied out of habit... not noticing that the rope was acting as my personal anchor." Another member of the party noted that, for himself, "even when he builds the master point with the rope, he prefers to not anchor himself with the rope, because making sure you don't unanchor yourself is one more thing to worry about when you're setting up rappels and lowers." Good habits are important, and it can be helpful to rely on the same proven and well-understood anchoring system. However, climbers confront a host of variables—available tools, weather, rock quality, other climbers—and safety is best served with a flexible set of methods that may be effective across a broad spectrum of scenarios. Whatever anchoring method is chosen, it's important to follow a generalized set of safety checks. As the leader noted, "I learned from this to take an extra moment to check myself when deviating from my usual patterns, and also to make an extra check whenever untying." (*Sources: Anonymous report and the Editors.*)

Belayer at the exposed stance atop the second pitch of Baby. Three people crowded this small stance during the near miss described here. *Rob Painten*

SHAWANGUNKS ANNUAL SUMMARY
Mohonk Preserve

In 2018 there were 23 reported climbing-related accidents. Injuries included five traumatic head injuries, one spinal fracture, several long-bone fractures, three open fractures of the lower legs, and minor ankle, wrist, shoulder, and hand injuries. Thirteen accidents required technical rescue, including six high-angle rescues. Two fatalities occurred after climbers fell a distance of greater than 60 feet to the ground.

Two climbers were injured when a top-rope anchor system failed on Herdy Gerdy (5.6) in the Trapps. One of the climbers fell around 20 feet to the ground, landing on another person sitting at the base. The climber suffered fractured vertebrae, and both suffered additional minor injuries. Upon inspection, Mohonk Preserve rangers found that the climber had set up the top-rope using hardware store webbing for the anchor system and clothesline as the belay rope.

While attempting to lead Nice 5.9 in the Trapps, a climber fell and suffered a traumatic brain injury. The climber had only placed two pieces of protection during the climb, the first about ten feet off the ground and the second at roughly 25 feet. The climber fell at the crux, and the higher piece failed to hold, resulting in an uncontrolled fall to the ground. The climber was wearing a hard-shell helmet.

A climber suffered kneecap, lower leg, and wrist fractures after a ground fall from the top of the "AMC Slab" in the Trapps. The climber was untethered to a safety system while cleaning the anchor site. Damp conditions at the time caused the rock to be slick.

A climber died after suffering multiple systems trauma in an uncontrolled fall of approximately 80 feet from Grand Traverse Ledge. The climber and their partner had just completed the first pitch of Arrow (5.8) in the Trapps and swapped gear on the GT Ledge. A decision was made to build a new anchor below the second pitch, which required a short walk across the ledge. Still tied in but not belayed, the climber lost their footing and fell off the ledge. The partner attempted to arrest the fall by grabbing the rope and sustained third-degree burns to the hands in the attempt.

Another fatal fall took place in the High Exposure area of the Trapps. The fall was not witnessed by climbers, so the exact climb being attempted and the cause are unknown. Inspection by Mohonk Preserve rangers found the climber wearing a harness with an ATC attached, along with a rope coiled and tied to the back. This suggests the climber intended to use the rappel stations nearby for descent upon completing a route. The absence of any additional gear suggested the climber had been free soloing.

In the Peters Kill area, a climber suffered a traumatic open fracture of the right ankle when an accident occurred during a top-rope lower. The climber had completed a 5.6 route on the Bunk Bed Wall and asked the belayer to lower him. The belayer fed rope out before ensuring the climber's weight was on the system. Upon leaning back, the climber fell about 15 feet before the belay held, resulting in an impact with a ledge. Once on scene, Mohonk Preserve rangers found the climber sitting on a small ledge about 40 feet up, still tied into the top-rope system. The belayer had disconnected the belay in an attempt to scramble up the cliff to provide aid. Rangers secured the patient to an anchor system, provided care, and executed a high-angle rescue.

A climber suffered a traumatic brain injury after a fall on Anguish (5.8) in the Trapps. Starting the third pitch, the climber fell approximately 20 feet before the belay caught and swung the climber into the cliff face. The climber was unresponsive while hanging below the belayer. The partner tied off the system and contacted emergency services. Once on the scene, rangers found the patient had regained consciousness but was unable to communicate. Rangers hauled the patient to Grand Traverse Ledge and then moved a short distance to the anchors on Three Pines (5.3) for lowering. The climber's foam helmet had broken in several places in the fall.

While leading the second pitch of Modern Times (5.8+) in the Trapps, a climber suffered injuries to the rib cage during a fall. The climber was approximately 20 feet diagonally up from the last piece of protection, resulting in a large pendulum swing into the cliff. Rangers stabilized the climber's injuries and lowered them from Grand Traverse Ledge to the ground.

ANALYSIS

Several accidents in 2018 likely would have had much worse outcomes if climbers were not wearing a helmet at the time they fell. Additionally, several accidents might have been avoided completely if climbers had been attached to a safety line or been on belay in exposed locations. In several accidents, additional protection could have mitigated the damage from falls when the last piece of protection failed to hold. (*Source: Andrew Bajardi, Chief Ranger of the Mohonk Preserve.*)

NORTH CAROLINA

GROUND FALL | Inexperience, Inadequate Belay
Pilot Mountain State Park, The Parking Lot

Late in the afternoon on May 9, Dylan Pappas (21) fell to the ground while climbing Chicken Bone (5.8), a ten-bolt sport route. A member of his climbing party had led the climb before him and left the draws in place. The third bolt was clipped with a shortened sling (an "alpine draw"), with which Dylan had no experience. A witness stated that while attempting to clip this draw, about 25 feet up, it appeared Dylan was "fiddling with his sling and carabiner." He accidentally removed the lower carabiner from the sling and then, when he attempted to reclip it, he did so incorrectly. When Dylan weighted the rope, the lower carabiner pulled free from the sling.

A climber below Chicken Bone at Pilot Mountain, showing the bolt where another climber incorrectly clipped a quickdraw and fell to the ground. *Pilot Mountain State Park*

Dylan yelled "falling" and his belayer, Alex, initially was unsuccessful at arresting the fall, as he did not have control of the brake strand in his tube-style belay device. The belayer finally gained control, but Dylan impacted the ground in a partially seated position before hitting his head on the ground and losing consciousness. Dylan was wearing a helmet. After a night in the hospital for monitoring, he was released the next day with a bruised tailbone. (*Sources: Pilot Mountain State Park rangers and Doug Lutz, Fox Mountain Guides.*)

ANALYSIS
When used properly, extendable slings can reduce rope drag and minimize the chance of traditional protection pieces pulling out. In this case, the sling was configured properly but used incorrectly by Dylan. Additionally, the belay was inadequate. Had the belayer been paying closer attention, he may have had time to lock off the brake strand before the climber hit the ground. (*Source: Aram Attarian.*)

FALL ON ROCK | Inexperience, No Helmet
Pilot Mountain State Park, Black Rain Wall

On November 1 at approximately 2 p.m., my partner and I were climbing in the Little Amphitheater when two climbers came around the trail in a hurry and obvious state of distress. Climber 1 (male, early 20s) was shirtless with his hands on his head and blood streaming down his head and face. There were numerous abrasions on his torso. I immediately lowered my climbing partner to the ground, and a nearby pair of climbers came over to assist. One of them was a doctor. I retrieved my first-aid kit from my pack and the doctor donned gloves and attended to Climber 1's head injury. He had a severe laceration on his scalp but seemed alert and responsive. Very eager to get to the hospital, Climber 1 and Climber 2, his belayer (male, early 20s), were still wearing climbing shoes and had left all of their gear behind. My partner and I retrieved their walking shoes and offered to collect their gear while they went to the hospital.

The two had been attempting Black Rain, a 5.9 sport route. Earlier in the day, we had climbed the same route, which has six bolts and a large intermediate ledge. Many of the routes that day were wet from recent rains and mist. While we were able to send the route, we struggled to find good stances on the slippery rock, and my hand popped off several times, resulting in moderate lead falls.

ANALYSIS
Based on what we saw when we retrieved their gear, Climber 1's fall occurred above the ledge while attempting to clip the fourth bolt. Based on his description, he fell while clipping, landed on the ledge and struck his head (he was not wearing a helmet), then fell off the ledge. While cleaning their gear we noticed that several of the quickdraws were not clipped in the safest manner, including one that was back clipped. Overall, we got the sense that these two climbers were inexperienced and did not understand the risks inherent in climbing. Weather and conditions can greatly increase the difficulty of climbs and should always be considered in route choice. (*Source: Alexander "Sasha" Timkovich.*)

FALL ON ROCK | Protection Pulled, Impact on Ledge
Pisgah National Forest, Looking Glass Rock

Andrew Gatlin (24) and I, Peter Magnin (24), hiked in to climb at the North Side of Looking Glass Rock during the morning of September 21. We decided to attempt Invisible Airwaves. I started leading and was a majority of the way up the 80-foot first pitch (5.10c) when my foot slipped and I fell approximately 12 to 15 feet. During the fall, my right foot impacted a small ledge about three to five feet below me, and two small cams (a yellow 0.8 Totem and a 0.4 Black Diamond X4) in shallow placements above the ledge blew, causing me to fall an additional ten feet. My right ankle began to swell immediately, and I was lowered to the ground. I'm a Wilderness EMT, and with my training and Andrew's help, I was able to splint the ankle. It took us about 1.5 hours to hike out. I went to the hospital where an X-ray revealed no fractures.

ANALYSIS
I should have looked for better gear placements. I had placed four pieces in the first 30 feet, got to a small traverse, and then placed two additional cams (1 and 0.75 Black Diamond), both of which were super-secure in a nice crack directly underneath the cams that blew. Careful placement of gear (especially small cams) along with doubling up pieces when placements are not ideal can help prevent dangerous falls. (*Source: Peter Magnin and the Editors.*)

ESSENTIALS

SPEAK UP
INTERVENING EFFECTIVELY FOR SAFER CLIMBING

By Ron Funderburke

Have you ever seen a climber doing something unusual, like belaying with an unfamiliar device or technique?

Have you ever seen a situation that may not be immediately dangerous but could be one day, like setting up a rappel device with a non-locking carabiner?

Have you ever seen an impending accident, like a belayer repeatedly dropping the brake strand of the rope to shoot photos of the leader at a crux?

Any of these scenarios might cause an experienced climber to feel concern, and some climbers might be tempted to intervene and try to stop or correct the behavior. But when is it actually appropriate to intervene and how can it be done in the most effective way? Intervention exposes a fellow climber to potential embarrassment, and it exposes the intervener to retaliation.

Consider that most people are not intentionally dangerous. Most people deserve the benefit of the doubt. In addition, many people have experienced interventions negatively, and, for good reason, they may be reflexively defensive.

It's hard to make sound judgments about safety without risking being a hypocrite. Most of us occasionally do things that could be safer. Some of us don't wear helmets at "safe" crags. Some of us don't use backups all the time. Effective safety interventions require the intervener to have some perspective on the severity of hazard, in order to modulate the severity of the response.

The first question to ask yourself before intervening with fellow climbers is this: "Is harm imminent?" If the answer is yes, an urgent intervention is justified. If not, or if you're not sure, a softer approach is often more appropriate.

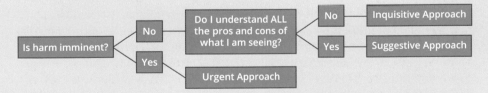

INQUISITIVE APPROACH

Some things you see at the crag are not necessarily unsafe, just unfamiliar or unusual. For an intermediate or experienced climber, this may provoke a desire to intervene with a "better" method. But it's also possible that an unfamiliar or unusual technique might actually be cutting edge. Or it might be an equally effective technique that's just different from the one you were taught. Do you really understand all the pros and cons of what you're seeing? A soft intervention helps the intervener discern the difference between novelty and naïveté.

Consider the example of a belayer using an unfamiliar device. You're curious and just a little concerned. If the belayer knows exactly what he's doing, you want to learn more about it. If he doesn't know what he's doing, you want to offer to help.

The inquisitive approach would be to ask something like, "Hey, do you mind if I watch you use that belay device? I've never seen that one." Hopefully this will lead to a discussion and some information sharing. If the belayer can confidently demonstrate the unfamiliar device or technique, you'll learn something. If he or she appears unconfident or inept with the belay, it may be time to ramp up the intervention.

SUGGESTIVE APPROACH

This approach may be appropriate when you see things that aren't exactly best practice, but don't imply imminent harm either. A reasonable and humbly presented suggestion can be persuasive. For example, take the climber about to rappel with a device clipped to her harness using a non-locking carabiner. Nine times out of ten, no harm would result, but it's clearly not the best practice.

"Excuse me," you might say. "Sorry, I don't mean to interrupt, but I was wondering about your rappel setup."

Climber: "What do you mean?"

"I mean your carabiner. Do you typically use a non-locker? I tend to use a locking carabiner right there."

At this point, some climbers won't be willing to listen, and they may even respond with something dismissive or derogatory. But if they open a door, you can have a useful conversation.

Climber: "I'm not sure. I've only done this a couple times."

"Cool," you say, "I was just asking because it's really more secure to use a locking carabiner to connect the device to your belay loop. Do you need to borrow one?"

URGENT APPROACH

Some situations are genuinely urgent. If harm is about to occur, act decisively to prevent someone from getting hurt. Feelings and egos can be salvaged afterward. To avoid overstepping, quickly ask yourself: Do I really understand what I'm seeing, and is it imminently dangerous? If the answer to both questions is yes, don't be afraid to act.

That belayer dropping the brake hand to shoot photos of his shaky leader? This is probably a case where asking questions and making suggestions isn't enough—a ground fall may be imminent. You could grab the rope behind the belayer to back up the belay or tie an overhand on a bight as a temporary backup. You'll likely have a pissed-off belayer on your hands, but you also might have saved someone's life.

WE'RE ALL IN THIS TOGETHER

Tactful and precise interventions take practice, so don't lose heart if your first attempts instigate unsavory interactions. Incrementally, you'll get better at intervening, and we'll all get better at experiencing an intervention. We're all in this together. If we're reflexively giving each other the benefit of the doubt, then we'll be patient when others are impatient, and we'll be delicate when others are indelicate.

Ron Funderburke is education director of the American Alpine Club.

GROUND FALL | Inadequate Protection
Hanging Rock State Park, Moore's Wall

Late in the afternoon on October 13, JLC (22) fell approximately 30 feet while leading the traditional route Breaking Rocks Is Hard to Do (5.9). JLC stated that he had been climbing for several years and had led the route before. He was 15 feet above his second piece of protection and getting ready to place a third when he "lost his grip" and fell. This resulted in a ground fall, with JLC landing on his back and fracturing three ribs. He was wearing a helmet. Local rescue squads were staged in the park for a scheduled trail race and were able to quickly assess his injuries and evacuate him. (*Source: Hanging Rock State Park rangers.*)

ANALYSIS
The opening moves of this route are strenuous but can be protected well. Placing additional gear while close to the ground or above ledges is advisable. By wearing a helmet, the climber likely prevented a more serious injury. (*Source: Aram Attarian.*)

FALL ON ROCK | Inexperience, Inadequate Protection
Linville Gorge Wilderness, The Daddy

On Saturday, October 27, a trio of climbers (James, Markus, and Jason), all from the Atlanta area, arrived at the base of the Daddy (5.6), located in the Amphitheater. Jason (46) was a relatively new trad climber being mentored by James, who was the most experienced of the three. Jason had experience in climbing gyms.

Jason stated, "I took the lead on the first pitch, since it appeared to be an easy climb. We weren't planning to return to the base of Daddy, so we were carrying everything up with us. In hindsight, I was carrying a lot more weight than I was accustomed to, and it likely threw off my balance.

"I tied in and started to climb, with Markus belaying. Approximately 10 feet up, I started to look for somewhere to set my first pro. I saw a really good spot that required just one more move. As I moved upward, my right foot slipped. Next thing I knew, I was falling. Markus was spotting me—I never put in my first piece, so I was never actually on belay—and he caught me as best he could and sat me down on the ground. He and James quickly looked me over, but I knew things weren't good when I saw bone."

Landing on uneven ground caused Jason's foot to roll, resulting in an open fracture of the lower leg. The group attempted unsuccessfully to use a cell phone to call 911, and then James was able to make contact with hikers on the ridge above who called for medical assistance. Because of his injury and location, a helicopter rescue was required. Jason was managed for 4.5 hours and had to be moved 300 meters downhill to a better pickoff point. However, rescuers noted that if the helicopter had not been used, the evacuation would have required an estimated 14 hours.

ANALYSIS
Jason noted: "Next time I'll place protection earlier, especially when the ground below the climb is as uneven as it is at the base of the Daddy. Also, we'll never overload the lead climber with gear. The followers can carry the leader's extra gear. (*Sources: Jason Januzelli and James Robinson and Adrian Hurst of Burke County Rescue.*)

OREGON

FATAL FALL | Failure to Self-Arrest, Inadequate Equipment
Mt. Hood, South Side

On February 13, Miha Sumi, 35, lost his footing near the summit of Mt. Hood while descending a south side route, resulting in a 700-foot fall. He was equipped for a snowboard descent (soft boots and self-arresting ski poles), resulting in his inability to self-arrest. The climber had an ice axe on his backpack and wore strap-on crampons on his boots in difficult surface conditions (hard snow and ice). Fellow climbers who went to Sumi's aid were threatened by falling ice and rocks as the day warmed. A Portland Mountain Rescue (PMR) team responded but was unable to revive the climber.

ANALYSIS
For hard snow or ice, proper footwear (rigid mountaineering boots with steel crampons) is needed for kicking steps and effectively using crampons. An ice axe is a better choice than self-arresting ski poles in such conditions. When self-arrest is doubtful, a rope and running protection should be used to safeguard against a fall. (*Source: Jeff Scheetz, Portland Mountain Rescue.*)

SKI MOUNTAINEERING FALL | Failure to Assess Conditions
Mt. Hood, South Side

At approximately 10 a.m. on May 26, an experienced skier (male, 35), attempted a ski descent of the Mazama Chute on the upper south slopes of Mt. Hood after reaching the summit. Following many days of warm conditions, the night of May 25 had been colder, with temperatures below freezing on the upper mountain. The snow surface was hard frozen corn—very firm and difficult to ski. According to witnesses, after two or three turns the subject fell and lost both skis. He tumbled about 400 feet, the full distance from Mazama Chute to Hot Rocks.

Hot Rocks was still partially covered with snow, and the upper transition from snow to rock consisted of multiple transverse crevasses. The subject flew across the first large crevasse, then fell vertically 20 feet off an ice edge, coming to rest in a trough on a snow shelf. He experienced extensive injuries from the fall and narrowly missed sliding off the shelf to the rocks below. His final location was precarious, with precipitous drop-offs just three feet from his landing point. His skis were lost in a crevasse.

Other climbers who witnessed the fall called 911. A team of four rescuers from Portland Mountain Rescue (PMR) was on the mountain that morning, and they reached the subject around 11 a.m. By that time, others climbers were assisting the injured climber, including an internal medicine resident from a local hospital.

The climber's location at the edge of an ice cliff above an active fumarole complicated evacuation and required more rigging and rescue personnel than the initial four rescuers could provide. While waiting for a larger team to arrive, the PMR team set anchors above and rigged a rope system that could be used to pendulum a litter and attendants across steep snow immediately above the ice cliff.

Attempts to recover the patient with a helicopter from an Oregon Army National Guard unit were thwarted by wind and turbulence. Instead, the patient was evacuated by penduluming the litter across a snow slope to the Hogsback. From there, rescuers lowered the litter some 1,500 feet to where it could be managed by unassisted litter attendants. The injured climber was transferred to a snow cat at the top of the Palmer lift at approximately 7 p.m. and then transported to Timberline Lodge, where he was loaded into a helicopter for transport to Portland.

ANALYSIS

Skiing off Mt Hood's summit is a common objective for expert skiers. However, conditions on the upper crater are often not appropriate, safe, or fun for a ski descent. On this day, the subject and his companion climbed to the summit and waited for the snow to soften. Unfortunately, they judged the snow condition in the couloir based on the exposed snow on top, which was not representative of the snow in the shaded chutes through the crater wall. Rather than confirming the snow had softened in the chute, the subject dropped in from above, only to find he could not hold an edge. He was unable to arrest the resulting fall. (*Sources: Mark Morford, Portland Mountain Rescue; rescuer observations; and the injured skier.*)

FALL ON SNOW | Inexperience, Inadequate Equipment
Mt. Hood, South Side

On May 28 a roped party of three climbers was descending the Pearly Gates at approximately 8:30 a.m. when one climber fell, pulling the others into an uncontrolled fall. No anchors or running protection were being used at the time of the fall.

The top climber (male, 50), who was the leader of the party, had wrapped excess rope around his body in a Kiwi coil configuration but had failed to tie off the working end of the rope at his harness. During the fall, the leader became wedged in a crevasse (southeast of the bergschrund) creating a virtual "dead man" anchor for the rope team. Had the leader not become snagged in the crevasse, the entire rope team would have fallen another 400 to 500 feet down the mountain.

After the fall was arrested, the leader was wedged in the upper crevasse, complaining of pain and unable to extract himself. Climber 2 (female, 48) lost a boot and crampon but reported that she was okay (she was later found to have a clavicle fracture), and Climber 3 (female, 48) was caught on the lip of a lower crevasse with an apparent head injury. All three came to a stop on a 50° slope and were unable to move.

Position of three climbers after a fall in the Pearly Gates area. All three had to be rescued, and one required a helicopter evacuation. *Portland Mountain Rescue*

A Portland Mountain Rescue (PMR) rescuer who had just begun descending the mountain was able to respond immediately, initiating a call for additional resources and coordinating a response with two mountain guides who volunteered to assist. Communication with the fallen climbers was difficult, as only two of the three climbers spoke any English and this was minimal.

One guide worked to secure the team's rope with a solid anchor to support the other climbers, extract the leader from the crevasse, and assess and treat his injuries. The second guide assisted climber 2, who did not feel confident unclipping from the rope system. Her missing boot and crampon were recovered by other climbers and returned to her. The PMR rescue leader attended to Climber 3, who was disoriented with a possible head injury. When assessing Climber 3, the rescuer identified that she was clipped into the rope with a non-locking carabiner and her harness was improperly buckled. Had the carabiner or harness failed, this climber could have fallen an additional 400 feet or more.

Rockfall and falling ice were assessed to be an immediate threat to life, thus the patients had to be moved out of the hazard zone as safely and expeditiously as possible. Climber 2 was lowered first. A solid anchor was rigged above her and offset from the edge of the crevasse below her, allowing the patient to be pendulumed around the crevasse and then lowered down the headwall and out of danger. Climber 3 was lowered on the same system as Climber 2. The PMR rescue leader then returned to the apex of the Hogsback and found the assisting mountain guide attempting to lower Climber 1 down the Hogsback. This climber did not speak any English but was clearly very cold and in great pain from apparent back and shoulder injuries. Climber 1 was lowered another 25 to 50 feet to remove him from the highest risk of falling objects. At that point, a shelf was cut into the slope to stabilize the patient.

Due to the severity of Climber 1's injuries, an Army Medevac Blackhawk helicopter was requested to hoist him from the scene. He was flown from the Hogsback to a nearby hospital for treatment. Climbers 2 and 3 descended the mountain with rescuers. The assistance of the two mountain guides, as well as many other climbers who donated personal climbing gear and clothing, made a big difference in the rescue. All should be commended for their time and generosity.

ANALYSIS

These climbers clearly lacked the expertise and experience for this route. In addition to the unsafe use of a rope and harness described above, witnesses reported that their technique while descending was poor. The climbers did not carry adequate gear to stabilize and protect each other from the elements if an accident occurred, requiring other climbers to donate clothing and gear to support them during the rescue. One climber had medical conditions requiring them to take prescription medications, which they had reportedly not taken within the last 24 hours. They were uncertain of the name of the medication or dose, further complicating the rescue.

The lack of English made it challenging for rescuers to assess and coordinate the rescue. PMR asked the sheriff to find a translator, and they located a tourist at Timberline Lodge who had a relative in New York who was able to assist. A teleconference using speakerphone was then used to interview the patient. This revealed important medical information, making the effort to locate a translator well worthwhile.

Lastly, this is a good illustration of when moving a trauma patient may be necessary. Though all patients had significant injuries, rocks falling by the patients were life threatening, so the decision to move the patients out of the hazard zone was appropriate. The patients were moved as little as possible and only to the extent necessary to remove them from the hazard zone. (*Source: Steve Rollins, Portland Mountain Rescue.*)

FALL WHILE DESCENDING | Tool Pulled Out of Ice
Mt. Jefferson

In the midafternoon of July 20, Sam Lowry (age 60) and I (Jon Sprecher, age 64) climbed the Jefferson Park Glacier route and were descending the North Milk Creek snowfield to loop back to our camp via the Russell and Jefferson Park glaciers. This descent is usually done unroped for speed, because the climbing is not too hard and if you're not placing protection you'd only pull off the other climber if you fell. It was late in the season and the surface was soft ice with patches of slushy sno-cone ice, making face-out descent difficult due to the variable conditions. I was descending face-in, using two tools, a Black Diamond Raven ice axe and a Chouinard alpine hammer.

Rescue helicopter approaches a climber on Mt. Jefferson after his night out with a broken leg. *Caleb Glaser/Ricky Yunke, Linn County Search and Rescue*

My accident occurred when, after I'd pulled out my axe to move down, the alpine hammer sheared in the soft ice and I started sliding and rotating to the right. My right crampon stuck in some ice, twisting my ankle and flipping me sideways. I flipped back over and self-arrested using the axe, stopping my slide after an additional 20 feet. I'd previously experienced a badly sprained ankle and quickly realized that I had a worse injury. I continued descending, kicking with one leg and "kneeing in" with the other before eventually crawling on my knees for several hundred more feet down to a point that was safe from rockfall. It was obvious that I wouldn't be able to complete the descent, so we called 911 on our one dying cell phone.

It was late in the day and we were forced to spend a night out, cold and sleepless. Still, with enough clothing, water, and food, it was "okay." The next afternoon, when we got tired of waiting for rescuers, my partner started down, and after an hour he ran into the search and rescue team ascending to find us; on his description of my injury, they called a helicopter for me. My injuries included a broken fibula and a couple of torn high-ankle ligaments.

ANALYSIS
If I'd had a second full ice axe, the pick likely would have gone in more deeply and not sheared out. I am very used to climbing with the Chouinard alpine hammer that I was using. Even so, next time I climb in the alpine I plan on using a medium length ice hammer with a longer pick. (*Source: Jonathan Sprecher.*)

FALL ON ROCK | No Helmet
Smith Rock, Dihedrals

On January 13, a female climber (34) was leading Karate Wall (5.12c R), a mostly bolted route with old-school runouts at the Dihedrals. The climber was above the next-to-last bolt, a few feet to the right of the bolt line, when she fell. She flipped upside down and hit her head on the wall, sustaining a head injury. She was not wearing a helmet. The climber had no rope burns on her legs and does not remember catching her foot on the rope. The belayer was able to lower the climber to the ground, and she was evacuated to medical care. (*Source: Deschutes County SAR.*)

ANALYSIS
While any number of things could have caused the climber to invert during her fall, a rope behind the leg is often the cause. Extra care should be taken to keep the rope in front of you while traversing. The climber and belayer report that they now both wear helmets. (*Source: Deschutes County SAR and the Editors.*)

FALL WHILE SCRAMBLING | Loose Rock, Haste
Smith Rock, Northern Point

On February 17, a male climber (30) fell while free soloing an "easy chimney" between the Lower Gorge and Northern Point. He was attempting a shortcut back to the parking lot after a day of climbing in the Marsupials, rather than taking the longer trail back. He had crossed the Crooked River and was attempting to find an old ladder made of rebar upstream of Northern Point while his party waited on the other side of the river to see if he was successful. Unable to find the ladder, the climber decided to attempt the chimney (which is not an established route). After approximately 20 feet, he encountered two chockstones and his backpack caught on one of these loose blocks. The block shifted onto his pack, pulling him off and causing him to fall. He first impacted a ledge at the base of the chimney and then fell another 20 feet before stopping on a sloping ledge. His friends immediately called 911, and Deschutes County SAR responded and performed a vertical raise to evacuate.

ANALYSIS
The subject stated that, in retrospect, he ignored his intuition, which was to back off and search for a better exit. The climber also stated that he was "a little too comfortable" in exposed terrain. It is important to take time to analyze potential hazards before committing to exposed terrain without a rope and to pay attention to time and social pressures that influence decision-making. Sometimes it is safer to take the long way out. (*Source: Deschutes County SAR.*)

STRANDED | Failure to Follow Descent Route
Smith Rock, Smith Rock Group, Northwest Face

Late on March 27, three male climbers (ages 24, 24, and 34) completed the popular five-pitch sport climb Wherever I May Roam (5.9). With darkness approaching and being unfamiliar with the established rappel route, the party mistakenly rappelled from the anchors at the top of the fifth pitch rather than the fixed anchor on the backside of the northwest wall. After reaching the anchors below, the party was not able to pull their rope, due to the friction of their rope traveling over the face above. They did not know how to ascend the rope and were stranded. The climbers contacted Deschutes County SAR, and a rescue team hiked up the backside of the northwest face, accessed the top of the climb, and assisted the subjects down the route. (*Source: Deschutes County SAR.*)

ANALYSIS
The guidebook for the area (*Rock Climbing: Smith Rock State Park*; Falcon Books) explicitly describes the descent route for this climb, and there are numerous descriptions of rappel and walk-off options listed on Mountain Project and other sites. (Photographing a guidebook description or saving webpages on a phone is a good way to carry essential descriptions without lugging a guidebook.) Climbers transitioning to multi-pitch routes need to be familiar with self-rescue skills and techniques not normally needed in single-pitch terrain, including the ability to ascend a stuck rope. Additionally, time management on long climbs is essential; approaching darkness can lead climbers to make hasty decisions. (*Sources: Deschutes County SAR and the Editors.*)

FATAL GROUND FALL | Slip On Exposed Terrain Above Climb
Smith Rock, Picnic Lunch Wall

On April 10, Alex Reed (20) was working on a new route on the Picnic Lunch Wall. He had hiked up Misery Ridge alone to access the top of the route, where the terrain is very exposed and requires some 4th- or 5th-class downclimbing. For unknown reasons, Reed fell an estimated 300 feet while attempting to access the top anchor, sustaining fatal injuries.

ANALYSIS
Reed was familiar with the terrain and had been there several times in the recent past while preparing the new route. It is believed that this was not a rappel error, but rather a slip in exposed terrain. As climbers it is important to consider the consequences of scrambling unroped or unanchored in exposed spots. The risk in this situation could have been mitigated by establishing an additional anchor above the exposed access point. (*Source: Deschutes County SAR.*)

STRANDED | Stuck Rappel Ropes
Smith Rock, Monkey Face, West Face

On May 15, two male climbers (ages 37 and 21), after having climbed Super Slab (5.6) on the Red Wall, attempted a shortcut to the base of the West Face Variation (5.8) on the west side of the Monkey Face to avoid hiking down the Misery Ridge Trail and around to the west face. They rappelled from anchors at the Springboard, a prominent ledge facing the Monkey Face, using two 60-meter ropes. These anchors are traditionally used for a Tyrolean traverse or slackline over to the Monkey Face, not for rappelling. When the two climbers reached the top of the first pitch of the West Face Variation, they were unable to pull the ropes due to friction on the rock,

and they did not know how to ascend the ropes. The party called 911 for help. Deschutes County SAR arrived on scene, and two members of the Mountain Rescue Team rappelled to the subjects and assisted them to the ground.

The slackline traverse from Misery Ridge to Monkey Face. Slackline anchors may be mistaken for rappel anchors. But their location often makes them unsuitable for rappelling. *Smithrock.com*

ANALYSIS

It is important for climbers to be able to recognize appropriate and inappropriate anchors for rappelling and to consider the effects of friction when pulling a rope. (*See page 52 for a similar incident with slackline anchors in Colorado.*) This party would have been better off walking to the base of their next route. Climbers attempting multi-pitch routes should have the skills and gear to ascend stuck rappel ropes if necessary. (*Source: Deschutes County SAR.*)

ROCKFALL | No Helmet
Smith Rock, West Side Crags, Mesa Verde Wall

On July 25, a male climber (48) was hanging from a fixed rope while cleaning a new route near the Mesa Verde Wall. The climber's rope dislodged a dinner plate–size rock from above that fell and struck him on the head. He was not wearing a helmet. The climber lowered to the ground where a friend called 911. The Deschutes County SAR team evacuated the injured climber using a wheeled litter. (*Source: Deschutes County SAR.*)

ANALYSIS

Rockfall must be anticipated when cleaning any new route. Wearing a helmet could have prevented or reduced the severity of head injury caused by the falling rock. When cleaning a new route, identifying loose rock to either side of the proposed line is a good idea as it might be dislodged by the rope or by climbers lowering off the route. (*Sources: Deschutes County SAR and the Editors.*)

GROUND FALL | Inexperience, Inadequate Protection
Smith Rock, Northern Point

On August 15, two male climbers (ages 32 and 47) were attempting Double Time, a 5.7 traditional route at Northern Point in the Basalt Rimrock area. After climbing approximately 30 feet, the leader fell, pulling out two cams (size unknown), and hit the ground. The climber was wearing a helmet.

ANALYSIS

It is believed the climber was new to traditional climbing, and that inexperience played a role in this incident. Before leading trad climbs, it's helpful to practice placing gear at ground level and have someone experienced evaluate the placements. Mock leading (protected by a top-rope) can also be helpful. This area of Smith Rock is easily accessed from the top and makes mock leads very practical. (*Source: Deschutes County SAR.*)

UTAH

STRANDED | Stuck Rappel Rope, No Headlamps
Wasatch Range, Big Cottonwood Canyon, Steorts' Ridge

Salt Lake County Search and Rescue got called out at 9:54 p.m. on May 3 for two climbers (male and female, both 20 years old) near the top of Steorts' Ridge. The pair had begun climbing the three-pitch 5.6 route around 5:50 p.m. At the top, they traversed down and left to reach the rappel route. (Anchors are in place for three rappels with a single 60-meter rope.) After making the first rappel, the climbers were unable to pull the rope—they had forgotten to untie a stopper knot—and decided to call for help.

A rescue team climbed up an alternative descent route to reach the rappel anchors. The stranded climbers didn't have any light source, and it was difficult to determine exactly where they were on the route in the dark without a visual. However, eventually they were reached and assisted down the route safely. Everyone was off the mountain around 4 a.m. (*Source: Salt Lake County Search and Rescue.*)

ANALYSIS
The gear packed for any multi-pitch route should include headlamps for each climber, especially when starting a route late in the day. (If you're not carrying a pack, modern lightweight headlamps can easily be clipped to a harness gear loop.) The rappel route for this buttress is notorious for snagging ropes, and there is an alternative descent with just a single rappel that many consider to be easier and safer. A few minutes of online research should be part of the plan before any long climb; the comments sections of online route descriptions often hold useful beta that doesn't appear in guidebooks. (*Source: The Editors.*)

RAPPEL ERROR
Wasatch Range, Big Cottonwood Canyon, Storm Mountain

On July 7, a male climber in his 20s fell to the ground while rappelling from a multi-pitch sport route called Addis Ababa (two pitches, 5.7). The climber and two partners had finished the route, and two of the three climbers had completed the rappels when they saw the third fall from near the first-pitch anchors to the ground.

The patient had open fractures in both legs and a head injury, among other injuries. Rescuers lowered him down low-angle terrain for about 100 feet, and then he was carried to Life Flight for a trip to a local hospital. (*Source: Salt Lake County Search and Rescue.*)

ANALYSIS
It's not clear what caused the fall, but rescuers believe the climber loaded his ATC-style rappel device incorrectly. Weight-testing the rappel setup before unclipping from the anchor could have prevented a fall resulting in many serious injuries. (*Source: The Editors.*)

LOWERING ERROR | Dangerous Swing While Cleaning
Wasatch Range, Big Cottonwood Canyon, Lonely Challenge Area

In early afternoon on September 25, Salt Lake SAR was called out to the Challenge Buttress after a male and female climber were involved in a climbing accident on Watermelon Tetris (5.9) at the Lonely Challenge sector. This 70-foot sport climb leans strongly to the right, making it difficult to clean the quickdraws from the top down. It was reported that while the male climber was being lowered from the anchors, he clipped his harness to the belayer's strand of the rope to keep close to the line of bolts as he removed the quickdraws. At some point he unclipped the other strand and lost or let go of it; the climber swung off and pulled his belayer off the ground, causing both of them to collide with the wall. The male had what appeared to be a minor head injury, but both were able to walk out with assistance. (*Source: Salt Lake County SAR.*)

When cleaning a steep sport route, always unclip from the belayer's rope *before* cleaning the lowest bolt to avoid dragging the belayer as you swing off. *Courtesy of Petzl*

ANALYSIS

Routes that are significantly overhanging or lean sharply to one side are best cleaned by a climber following the route, rather than the leader lowering from the top. When this is not possible (if the second cannot follow the climb, for example), care must be taken to prevent dangerous swings or sudden drops while cleaning. If the lowering climber clips into the rope strand running through the quickdraws to stay closer to the bolt line—sometimes called "tramming in"—the belayer must be braced for a sudden load in the system each time the climber cleans a draw. Also, the climber must take care to unclip from the belay strand *before* cleaning the lowest bolt or else the belayer may be dragged across the ground by the resulting swing. Consider a ground anchor for the belayer.

It's often preferable to leave the first bolt clipped when cleaning a steep sport pitch. The climber can then swing off the route a safe distance above the ground or can continue lowering to the ground with the belay strand still clipped. (Be aware that lowering all the way to the ground with the first bolt clipped requires additional rope. Tie a stopper knot.) Once the climber is on the ground, someone can climb back to the first bolt or use a stick clip to retrieve the gear. Again, the safest technique is to follow the pitch and clean it. (*Source: The Editors.*)

LEADER FALL | Inadequate Protection
Wasatch Range, Little Cottonwood Canyon

On Monday, June 11, my wife and I (male, age 31) went out for a casual day of climbing in Little Cottonwood Canyon. We headed up for a lap on Stifler's Mom (multi-pitch

5.11a), which we have climbed several times. Finding the route empty, we cruised on up, linking pitches and having a good time. My wife and I noted that the route seemed a bit dirtier than usual, probably from spring runoff.

I climbed through the sixth-pitch crux overhang feeling good. I clipped the bolt over the roof and worked my way up the thin but relatively easy corner above, admittedly not paying very close attention to the climbing in front of me. I noticed that a pin that used to be about halfway up the corner was no longer there. In its place, I plugged a red C3 Camalot, gave it a tug, and visually verified good contact on all the lobes. After climbing a little higher, with the C3 just below my feet, I fell.

I still don't know exactly why I slipped. I tried to run backwards down the slab but tripped over something—maybe the roof or the rope. I flew over the roof and landed on the slab below, about 10 feet below my wife at the belay ledge, facing downward, on my right shoulder. My head whiplashed against the rock and I slid another few feet before the rope caught me. In total the fall was roughly 30 to 35 feet. The C3 had popped, and the bolt that caught me was about eight feet below that placement.

I knew immediately that I'd been badly hurt. I could not command my diaphragm to move for nearly 10 seconds. Suddenly I was able to take shallow breaths, and I screamed up to my wife that I was alive but needed help. She tried to lower me to a ledge about 20 feet lower, but stopped when I realized that I could not control my body at all and I had probably injured my spine. At that point she tied me off and focused on keeping me still while coordinating a way to get me off the wall.

Bryce and Tyler, climbing below us, witnessed the event; they quickly climbed to our position. Tyler called emergency services. Andy also saw the fall from a route just up-canyon and rappelled to the base of pitch five and then ascended a fixed line to reach me. The next hour or so was a bit of a blur for me. Bryce later recounted what happened:

"While the position [the climber] was in was incredibly painful, Tyler and I initially made the difficult decision not to move him, given the possible neck or spinal injury he had sustained.... [However], he and his wife both eventually decided that his position was unendurable, given the projected rescue ETA, and requested that we attempt some sort of stabilization....

"I attached several slings with a prusik to the climber's line and adjusted them to support his legs once horizontal. Using a double-length sling, we were able to secure a makeshift chest harness around the climber and attach it to my line..... Once in position, we instructed his wife to begin slowly lowering her husband to align his hips and shoulders, resting him horizontally across our knees. We slowly brought his lower half down and rolled him facing upright, Andy supporting his neck while I worked to keep his back straight. While we did this, a helicopter appeared, hovered close, then retreated. Tyler soon confirmed over the phone that a long-line hoist attempt would be made, and we were to keep the patient stable while a rescue crewman secured him in a body sling.

"About 15 minutes passed before the helicopter came into position over us and began lowering the crewman. We worked as carefully as possible to get the sling around the patient while minimizing the amount of neck and spine movement. Eventually, we were able to secure the patient in the sling and, after cutting him loose of our tethers, the crewman signaled the heli to move up and away from the wall. From fall to extraction, Tyler and I estimate about an hour and thirty minutes passed."

Rescue helicopter prepares to haul off a badly injured climber who fell from the sixth pitch of a route in Little Cottonwood Canyon. *Salt Lake County SAR*

At the hospital they determined that I had a slightly displaced C2 fracture and a non-displaced C3 fracture with no direct damage to the spinal cord. I did not need surgery, but I would be wearing a neck brace for up to three months. I had central cord syndrome, probably from hyperextension of the spinal cord during impact, and this led to poor control and weakness in my arms and hands, especially on my left side, but it was expected that I would make a recovery. Considering the location of the fractures, I am lucky not to be paralyzed or dead.

ANALYSIS

Ultimately, the accident was caused by three factors coming together:

(1) I fell in a dangerous spot. With a large roof below me, the chances of becoming inverted in a fall were high. Additionally, the low-angle slab below the roof was a hazard that I underestimated.

(2) The rock quality in the corner was poor and I failed to protect it adequately. Knowing that the piece I placed was unreliable, I should have doubled up on gear.

(3) Having just climbed through a difficult crux, I let my guard down on easier terrain, even though it was arguably a more dangerous spot and should have demanded more focus.

My helmet has a huge dent on the front right side where I impacted. If I had not been wearing it, I might be a vegetable right now. I also am now keenly aware of the fact that we were lucky to be climbing roadside in the Wasatch rather than in the backcountry. This was basically the best possible scenario for rescue five pitches up a route, and it still took about two hours. (*Source: Mike Marmar.*)

LEADER FALL ON ROCK
Little Cottonwood Canyon, Gate Buttress

In the late afternoon of October 7, a 23-year-old female was leading a route called Kermit's Wad (5.10a) when she fell near the fourth bolt. The route ascends a steep granite slab, and as she fell, her climbing partners said, she flipped upside down and struck her head on the wall and was knocked unconscious. She was wearing a helmet.

Her climbing partners lowered her to the base of the route and called 911. The woman had some head and face injuries but was able to walk down with assistance from Unified Fire, which was first on the scene. (*Source: Salt Lake County Search and Rescue.*)

ANALYSIS

It's not known exactly what caused the leader to turn upside down as she fell, but a foot or ankle tangled in the rope or striking a ledge or foothold as she slid down the steep slab are likely culprits. This incident is a great reminder of the importance of wearing a helmet while climbing relatively "safe" routes such as single-pitch slabs. Though the patient apparently was briefly unconscious after striking her head, she might have suffered much more serious injuries if she had not been using a helmet. (*Source: The Editors.*)

LEADER FALL ON ROCK
Zion National Park, Moonlight Buttress

On April 4 at about 4:30 p.m., Zion dispatch received a report of climbers calling for help on the Moonlight Buttress climbing route. Rangers observed through binoculars that two climbers were at the top of the second pitch, one of whom (male, 60) appeared to have a splint on his ankle but otherwise did not appear to be seriously injured. The uninjured climber rappelled a fixed line to the ground, crossed the Virgin River, and walked to the road to speak with the rangers.

The party of two had been aid climbing the Moonlight Buttress route, planning to spend one night on the wall. The injured climber had fallen about four feet in ledgy terrain near the top of the third pitch, where there is mandatory 5.8 free climbing. He was wearing approach shoes, not climbing shoes.

The partner told rangers the climber's ankle was obviously deformed and angulated but not open. He said the injured climber would rappel but wanted his partner's assistance. Rangers gave him splinting supplies, a radio, and a 400-foot, 11mm rope for the rappel. The partner ascended his fixed line with the supplies and, since it was now getting dark, the pair decided to remain on the ledge until morning. A litter team and medic met the two at the base the next morning and carried the injured climber across the river to the road. (*Source: Andrew P. Fitzgerald, Zion National Park.*)

ANALYSIS
While aiding in climbing shoes is generally unattractive, it might be the best choice for a pitch with passages of difficult or awkward free climbing. (Another option is to change shoes mid-pitch.) Transitioning between aid and free climbing—e.g., moving in and out of aiders confidently—is a useful skill to practice before a big wall climb. (*Sources: Andrew P. Fitzgerald and the Editors.*)

VERMONT

AVALANCHE | Failure to Assess Conditions, Inadequate Equipment
Smugglers' Notch

On March 14, two instructors and four students of the Army Mountain Warfare School were ascending Easy Gully, a wide snow gully that rises from near the high point of the unplowed road through the notch, following a prominent landslide path. The gully rises at up to 40°. The Vermont Army National Guard team was participating in a rough-terrain training exercise that the Army has conducted in this area for many years. Easy Gully is also frequently used to approach several ice climbs above it.

At 1:05 p.m., as the team reached a point near fixed ropes the Army had installed near the start of the ice climb Grand Illusion, they triggered an avalanche. One team member was able to "swim" off to the side. Two slid 500 feet along the gully. Three others slid 1,000 feet and 50 feet vertically over a large rock. It is not known if any of the team members were roped together at the time. No one was carrying avalanche beacons, shovels, or probes.

Fortunately no one was completely buried and everyone was conscious. The team located everyone within 10 minutes. All were removed from the mountain within 1 hour 40 minutes by Army personnel. Five injured persons were then transported by local emergency services to the University of Vermont Medical Center. Injuries were reported to include fractures, contusions, and abrasions.

ANALYSIS

While there is no avalanche forecast for Smugglers' Notch, it would have been reasonable to assume the avalanche hazard was elevated. The snowpack's history was one of unseasonably warm weather followed by freezing, creating a sliding surface, and then several days of heavy snowfall. Two days prior to the Army incident, backcountry skiers triggered a significant avalanche in a nearby Smugglers' Notch gully that was reported on local television and in social media. On the day of the Army incident, the Smugglers' Notch Resort ski area reported 23 inches of snow in the previous 24 hours. The local climbing guidebook clearly states that many of the gullies in Smugglers' Notch, including specifically Easy Gully by name, are common locations for both natural and climber-triggered avalanches after recent snowfall. The specific site where the avalanche started is a natural collection point of snow coming off the cliffs above.

In follow-up investigations, the officers overseeing the training and the on-site instructors acknowledged they were overconfident in their assessment of the avalanche risk. Various faults in Army procedures—and failure to follow procedures—were noted. More thorough and honest communication among the extended team might have prevented this incident. The team was also overconfident in its ability to mitigate the risk. One day before the ascent, an instructor had attempted to reduce the avalanche risk by "... breaking the weak layer and knocking down snow from areas above Easy Gully

that have been known to trigger slides in the past." It is doubtful that a small amount of snow management could significantly reduce such high avalanche risk.

A cardinal rule of travel in avalanche-prone terrain is to expose only one person at a time to hazardous situations. In this incident, the entire six-person team was following each other in the gully at the same time. Although they were able to find and extricate all the avalanche victims, their lack of beacons, shovels, or probes could have had life-threatening consequences. (*Sources: Technical Report of U.S. Army Ground Accident* (redacted), *published reports, and the Editors.*)

Army team near the avalanche site in Easy Gully during a training exercise in 2015. *Tech. Sgt. Sarah Mattison*

GROUND FALL | Anchor Failure
Smugglers' Notch, Workout Wall

On December 27 at 1:30 p.m., Stephen Charest (39) was guiding an ice climbing group at the Workout Wall area in Smugglers' Notch. During the process of relocating a rope at the top of the cliff, the fixed anchor on which he was relying failed. He fell approximately 50 to 60 feet to the base of the cliff and suffered life-threatening traumatic injuries to his head, face, abdomen, and left extremities. He was wearing a helmet. Fellow guides, other climbers, and Smugglers' Notch Resort ski patrollers quickly reached him. He was evacuated 1.5 miles to the Jeffersonville trailhead by toboggan and transferred via a helicopter to the University of Vermont Medical Center.

ANALYSIS

The anchor consisted of two strands of accessory cord tied around a tree. Both strands failed. Inspection of the anchor after the accident showed that one strand was seriously frayed near where it had been joined in a knot around the tree. The other strand had a sharp cut where it entered the master-point knot. Neither of these defects appeared to be caused by the climber weighting the anchor. The degree to which he was unable to inspect the anchor, because of snow and ice in the area, is unknown. Charest is a very experienced climber, professionally certified guide, and co-owner of a climbing gym and mountaineering school, and this event is a sober reminder that accidents can happen to anyone.

Both loops of this anchor cord in Smuggler's Notch were compromised. *Vermont Dept. of Public Safety*

Fixed anchors may degrade due to many environmental factors. The integrity of accessory cords and webbing can be compromised due to sun or wind. Cordage may be cut or gnawed by animals. Ice tools and crampons can accidentally nick cords. Always inspect fixed anchors thoroughly, including behind and underneath anchor points and both sides of webbing and knots. If there is any doubt of an anchor component's strength and integrity, back it up. (*Sources: Tim Farr, Neil Van Dyke (Vermont Department of Public Safety), and the Editors.*)

LOWERING ERROR | Rope Too Short, No Stopper Knot
Bolton Quarry

On September 29, DP and JC (both age 23) were climbing Wandering the Halls, a 5.8+ sport climb, at Bolton. DP described himself as a novice climber; JC was the more experienced of the two. DP was top-roping, with JC belaying from a wide ledge at the start of the climb. DP trailed a second rope that was 50 meters long. When he reached the top of the climb, he cleaned the anchor and threaded the trailing rope through the rappel rings, and JC switched his belay from the lead rope to the trailing rope in preparation to lower DP. It was now dark; both climbers were using headlamps.

To attach himself to the trailing rope, DP tied a figure-8 on a bight somewhere near the middle of the rope and clipped this to his harness with a carabiner. This meant there was about 25 meters of rope between DP and his belayer available for lowering. The climb is approximately 15 meters high, which meant there was not enough rope to lower DP all the way to the bottom of the route. The climbers had failed to put a stopper knot at the end of the rope, so when the end reached JC, it passed through his belay device. DP fell to the ledge, then fell another three to five meters to the ground. He suffered multiple injuries, including a spinal fracture.

ANALYSIS

The primary causes of the accident were the climber tying into the middle of the rope instead of the end, which resulted in insufficient length to complete the lower-off, and the climbers failing to put a stopper knot in the other end of the rope to close the system. Either action likely would have prevented the accident. It is unclear why DP trailed a rope to lower off instead of simply using the rope with which he was top-roping. This decision added complexity to their rope management. In addition, finishing in the dark and using headlamps is not ideal for situational awareness. The late hour of the climb also may have led to a sense of urgency, resulting in some carelessness. (*Sources: Neil Van Dyke, Vermont Department of Public Safety and the Editors.*)

VIRGINIA

LOWERING ERROR | Rope Too Short, No Stopper Knot
Elizabeth Furnace, Buzzard Rocks

My partner and I were climbing at the Buzzard Rocks crag, a series of slabs at the top of a ridge. A hiking trail goes to the top and climbers have to either rappel or hike down a climber's trail to reach the base of the wall. As we were setting up to climb an adjacent route, we watched two climbers rappel Melungian Brotherhood (5.8). Person 1 (male, 17) rappelled using one doubled rope to an intermediate anchor, and then set up another rappel with a second rope to reach the base. We wondered why they hadn't just joined their ropes, but kept going about our business. Once they were both at the base and had retrieved their ropes, Person 2 (male, 17) prepared to lead the route. We assumed that he would be belaying from the top, since neither of their ropes had been long enough to reach the ground when doubled.

We went around the corner to our next route, and some time later heard a series of crashes as if someone had dropped a backpack off the side of the mountain. We went back around the corner to find Person 2 several feet downslope from the base trail, covered in blood, and Person 1 calling for help. I introduced myself as a WFR and began patient assessment while my partner headed for the trailhead to meet rescuers. Person 1 stayed on the phone with EMS.

Person 2 was wearing a helmet but had several head injuries, an ankle injury, and lots of abrasions. About an hour and a quarter after the fall, several sheriff's deputies arrived and took over the scene. Eventually a litter was brought, and about 30 people helped carry the litter out.

ANALYSIS

Person 1 said that he was lowering Person 2 and suddenly the rope flew through his hands. I have no doubt they ran out of rope and there was no stopper knot to close the system. They were using a 60-meter rope on a route that had required them to do two rappels. Both of them were relatively new climbers. Closing the system (e.g., a stopper knot or tying in the belayer's end of the rope) should be part of learning to belay, and should be checked before leaving the ground every time.

In hindsight, I wish we had not assumed they would belay from the top and had asked what they planned to do. In the future, my partner and I will probably be a bit more inquisitive around less experienced climbers. (*Source: BR.*)

LOWERING ERROR | Miscommunication
Richmond Area

On January 6, after a prolonged cold spell, my climbing partner (36) and I (33) checked to see if a small cliff that continuously seeps water had frozen into something climbable. We found a 30-foot wall of poorly bonded ice, with a free-hanging pillar that descended along the roots of hanging ivy from the top of the wall. We set up a top-rope anchor around a thick tree about 20 feet up the slope above the ice flow.

I top-roped the pillar and found it surprisingly stable. Upon reaching the top, I agreed to move the rope farther right, around a small corner, to better align the climber with another aspect of the ice flow. My partner and I did not communicate whether he would lower me or I would rappel. Unfortunately, I assumed that I would be lowered after I repositioned the rope, while my partner assumed I was going to rappel. We couldn't see one another, and we each were wearing multiple hood and hat layers, making it difficult to hear each other despite the relatively short distance between us.

Readying to lower and feeling some resistance on the climbing rope, I yelled to my partner, "OK!" My partner replied, "OK, I'm taking you off belay!" Unfortunately, I didn't hear him. Not hearing any objection and not detecting weight or movement in the rope, my partner proceeded to take me off belay. I took another step and leaned back. Suddenly I was airborne, falling 30 feet to the snow-covered rocks and frozen mud below. After hitting the ground, I slid 25 additional feet, headfirst on my back. My partner called 911, and eventually I was transported to a local trauma center, where I was diagnosed with three compression fractures, two broken right ribs, a broken right scapula, a broken left ankle (talus), and a concussion. Fortunately, I was wearing a helmet.

ANALYSIS

As a longtime climber, I can't attribute this accident to inexperience; rather, insufficient communication between partners was the root cause. In hindsight, we should have (1) clearly communicated the plan to lower or rappel for the next climb, (2) followed standard belay communications (i.e., the belayer waiting for an "off belay" command prior to taking the climber off, and (3) followed a clear communications protocol prior to weighting the rope to be lowered. (*Source: Rick DeJarnette, with assistance from belayer Dan Durst.*)

WASHINGTON

FATAL FALL ON SNOW | Party Separated, Possible Avalanche
Mt. Adams, South Spur

On May 27, about 12:30 p.m., a call came in to the Yakima County Sheriff's Department that a climber (Alexander Edward, 28) had fallen from around 11,000 feet on the south side of Mt. Adams. His two partners were ahead of the climber and did not see him disappear. Rescuers performed a helicopter search but had to stop due to high winds. On May 29, a skier reported finding a body in one of the snowy chutes on the southwest side of the mountain, at around 8,500 feet. Edward's remains were later recovered. (*Sources: Yakima County Sheriff's Department and published reports.*)

ANALYSIS
It's not known what caused the climber to fall. It is possible he had wandered off-route and either slipped on icy terrain or was caught in a snow slide; the skier reported seeing extensive avalanche debris in the area. No crampons were found with the body. It's normal to travel unroped on this moderate route, but climbers should try to stick together to prevent any team member from getting off-route or to help in case one climber is distressed. (*Source: The Editors.*)

BELAY ERROR | Rope Burns
Vantage, Frenchman Coulee

On June 12, Climber 1 planned a day of instruction and climbing at Frenchman Coulee for his friend, Climber 2, who had no experience climbing outside. Following instruction on knots, equipment, and belay techniques, Climber 1 provided on-the-spot feedback as Climber 2 belayed him on short, easy routes. Climber 2 verbalized and demonstrated proper belay technique with both a Grigri and an ATC-style device. Feeling comfortable with Climber 2's abilities, Climber 1 proposed a more difficult route. At approximately 1:20 p.m., Climber 1 fell while attempting to clip the last bolt on Ride 'Em Cowboy (5.9 sport, 70 feet). Climber 1 shouted "falling!" and Climber 2 mistakenly used his left hand to grab the rope exiting his ATC-style belay device and running up to the leader. The belayer regained control with his right (braking) hand and caught the fall after about 55 feet. The leader came to a stop at eye level with the first bolt on the route.

The leader instructed the belayer to lower him and immediately untied from the rope. They poured cool potable water on Climber 2's burns. (Climber 1 and Climber 2 are both trained emergency nurses and understood the gravity of the injuries.) The two self-rescued to a Level II trauma center, where the belayer was diagnosed with a full-thickness burn to the left index finger and partial-thickness burns to the other digits and palm of the left hand.

ANALYSIS
Climber 1 should have established a pre-climbing plan determining which routes would be suitable and produce the least likelihood of a fall on Climber 2's first outing. Further,

Climber 1 should have equipped Climber 2 with the assisted-braking device in lieu of the ATC. This might have prevented the uncontrolled fall and the burns to the belayer's hands. [*Editor's note: If the belayer holds tight with the guide hand on the climber's strand of the rope in a fall, this can partially or fully defeat the effectiveness of assisted-braking devices such as Grigris. Whatever device is used, the belayer must use the brake hand to control a fall.*] This situation also highlights the usefulness of belay gloves.

In the end, despite severe burns, Climber 2's ability to regain control of the belay prevented Climber 1 from a likely fatal impact with the ground. (*Source: Anonymous report from the climbers.*)

FATAL FALL ON SNOW | Fatigue, Failure to Self-Arrest
Cascades, Mt. Stuart, Cascadian Couloir

About 11:50 a.m. on June 24, a climber called 911 to report that his partner (Varun Sadavarte, 32) had fallen several hundred feet on Mt. Stuart and couldn't be reached. Sadavarte and Owen Thomas (37) were friends who had taken a mountaineering course the year before and had climbed Mt. Baker and Mt. Adams. At 4 a.m. on June 24, they left their campsite and started up the Cascadian Couloir, which has significant snow in early summer. They exited the couloir around 6:30 a.m. After ascending to the saddle between Stuart and Sherpa Peak, Sadavarte and Thomas hit the false summit a few hundred feet below the top.

The route ahead was steeper than Thomas was expecting, so he decided to wait while Sadavarte went to the summit. Sadavarte returned about 11 a.m. and said he was hungry and a little tired. He took a five- to ten-minute minute break for some food and water, and they started to discuss which way to descend. Sadavarte took three steps along the snow slope below their rest spot, lost his balance, and began sliding on his stomach. He fumbled with his ice axe but was unable to slow down and quickly disappeared from sight. Thomas called 911 after not being able to see or verbally contact his partner.

A climber below who had witnessed the slide yelled up to Thomas that he could see Sadavarte and he appeared to be unresponsive. Another climber was able to climb down to where Sadavarte had stopped. He also called 911 to report the accident and relay his opinion that Sadavarte had not survived the fall.

By 2:40 p.m., a helicopter crew from Naval Air Station Whidbey Island was on scene and confirmed the climber was dead. They hoisted his body into the helicopter at 3:25 p.m. and delivered it to a staging area before returning to the mountain to retrieve Thomas, who did not believe he could safely descend after witnessing his partner's fall. Searchers recovered Sadavarte's backpack and helmet, which sustained significant damage to the left side and front consistent with tumbling into a rocky basin. (*Source: Chelan County Sheriff's Department.*)

ANALYSIS
A few things likely contributed to this accident. Effectively using an ice axe to self-arrest might have prevented the fall. Fatigue also played a role. This is a long climb, gaining 4,600 feet from the campsite, and the climbers may have needed more time to rest and take in calories before descending a steep snow slope they'd already identified as potentially dangerous. (*Source: The Editors.*)

FALL ON ROCK | Broken Hold, Inadequate Protection
Mt. Thomson, West Ridge

On July 14, King County Sheriff's Search and Rescue was notified that Peter Keckemet (24) had fallen about 100 feet on the west ridge of Mt. Thomson and possibly had broken bones. A helicopter crew was able to pick up Peter and take him to Harborview Medical Center in Seattle, where he was diagnosed with a fractured vertebra and multiple contusions. Rescuers guided his partner (25) back to the trailhead.

The partner said Keckemet would have fallen only about 20 feet, but a piece of protection pulled loose and instead he fell about 70 feet onto a ledge. Keckemet was not responsive at first. His partner used an emergency beacon to call for help.

ANALYSIS
The west ridge of Thomson has three or four pitches of mostly fourth class and low fifth class, with a few 5.6 moves. Keckemet later said that a foothold had broken, causing his fall. It's tempting to run it out on easy ground, but placing an extra protection piece occasionally is cheap insurance—it takes little time and has shortened many potentially serious falls in the mountains. (*Sources: King County Sheriff's Department and published reports.*)

Editor's note: An excellent short video with a rescuer's eye view of this helicopter rescue is viewable at publications.americanalpineclub.org.

FALL ON ROCK | Inadequate Protection and Anchor
North Cascades, Washington Pass, Le Petit Cheval

On July 14, Alexis and I scrambled to the base of Spontaneity Arête (multi-pitch 5.7) on Le Petit Cheval. There were no photos on Mountain Project of the first pitch, so we weren't sure exactly where the route started. We scrambled up to a ledge below two crack options. Alexis tried the left one first, but the awkward offwidth seemed hard to protect and more difficult than 5.7. She downclimbed to our belay ledge and moved over to a hand and fist crack on the right. This crack took better gear, but she found it similarly awkward.

When Alexis was about 10 feet up the crack, we decided we should look for other options, perhaps further to the right. She started to downclimb again. When she was about four feet above the starting ledge, she took out the first cam she had placed. Then she lost her balance or slipped, and she fell.

I tried to spot her with my left arm, but it was a futile effort. And we had made a critical mistake: Since we were just starting the "first pitch" and were on a ledge, I hadn't anchored myself to belay. So, when she fell, we had zero protection and no anchor. With about five feet of rope between us and my MegaJul assisted-braking belay device in use, we were a connected duo, and we both went tumbling down. We fell over the 10-foot fourth-class scramble we'd done to reach our belay ledge and then rolled a bit more, miraculously managing to stop on a 30° dirt slope, after falling about 15 feet in all. There was a 50-foot drop below.

Alexis was a few feet below me, upside down. I called out her name, and at first she didn't respond, then mumbled a bit. I looked around to assess the situation. I needed to get us anchored. About six feet above me was a large tree. I stood up and felt pain in my left leg; when I pulled up my shorts, I found a large, bloody gash. "I'll deal with that later," I thought. I walked up to the tree and built an anchor, then identified a flat ledge that Alexis could lie on. She was repeating that she'd broken her wrist and her teeth; I knew she probably also had a concussion. I worried about a spinal injury, but in our precarious position, I decided she had to be moved—help would be hours away. Anchored to the tree and keeping her on belay, I was able to pull her upright, and we moved together up to the ledge.

We used our Garmin inReach to signal for help. While we waited, Alexis started to become coherent again, and I placed a SAM splint on her wrist and gave her pain pills. Another climbing group arrived at our location and helped out with food and morale. After about an hour and a half, a helicopter arrived and lifted us both out.

ANALYSIS

We actually had scrambled about 10 feet past the real start of the climb to reach the ledge where I belayed. Our bigger mistake was not placing a belay anchor. We felt secure on the ledge, but

The start of Spontaneity Arête. The climbers scrambled to a higher ledge to start pitch one, then fell past this point from their unanchored stance. *Andrew Leader*

since the terrain below was exposed, we should have been treating this as a multi-pitch scenario, in case someone fell below the "ground" of the first pitch.

Another mistake was how we handled the downclimb. Alexis could have simply left the lowest piece in and either lowered from it or used it as protection until she reached the ledge. We then could have built an anchor and/or placed more pro so we could safely climb back up to retrieve the cam. Or, even though it's a difficult decision, we could have just left a piece behind. *Editor's note: This party was well-equipped for an emergency, with an inReach and walkie-talkies for two-way communication with responders, as well as an effective first-aid kit.* (Source: Andrew Leader.)

FATAL SLIP DURING DESCENT | No Helmet
North Cascades, Forbidden Peak

About 3:50 p.m. on August 4, climbers used an inReach device to notify the North Cascades Communication Center that a man had fallen while descending Forbidden Peak and was in need of help. The man was later identified as Eric Lindblom (60). After a summit attempt on the west ridge, Lindblom and three others were descending unroped on moderately exposed slabs above their bivouac site in Boston Basin. The rock was wet from snowmelt and slippery. Lindblom lost his footing and fell about 90 feet, landing in a pool of glacier water. He survived the fall but was unconscious and had a fractured leg and severe skull fracture. He had removed his helmet shortly before his fall.

Park personnel gave the climbers instructions on how to care for Lindblom while a rescue attempt began. A helicopter crew arrived around 5 p.m., and Lindblom was pronounced dead just before 6 p.m., having never regained consciousness. (*Sources: North Cascades National Park incident reports and published accounts.*)

ANALYSIS

Accidents happen on the way to and from climbs, not just on the route. Wearing a helmet until the descent was completed could have meant a less tragic outcome. It's quite possible that fatigue and haste also played a role in the fall. A storm was moving in (rain, wind, and lightning hampered the rescue operation), and the team may have felt time pressure. Timeliness is often critical in the alpine, but in exposed terrain it's important to move cautiously, choose your route carefully, and rest frequently. (*Source: The Editors.*)

FORBIDDEN PEAK RESCUES: *The Navy search and rescue team based on Whidbey Island conducted two helicopter rescues on Forbidden Peak in the summer of 2018. On June 19, two climbers were hoisted from the mountain in a nighttime operation. On August 2, the Navy crew rescued a climber who had fallen at around 7,500 feet and was wedged between rock and ice with multiple fractures. Additional details were not available.*

RAPPEL ANCHOR FAILURE | Inadequate Anchor and Backup
Mt. Rainier National Park, Dewey Peak

On August 14, three climbers summited Dewey Peak, a 6,710-foot mountain on the east side of Mt. Rainier National Park with a third- or fourth-class route to the

Rappel anchor that failed on Dewey Peak. An investigation concluded the yellow cordelette around the block was held in place by the carabiners linking that cord to a backup cam (not seen). When the backup gear was removed, the cordelette slipped over the block as the last rappeller started down. *Climber 3 Photo*

top. The climbers had met earlier that year in a local climbing course, in which Climber 1 acted as a volunteer instructor and Climbers 2 and 3 were students with no previous experience. After summiting, Climber 1 first inspected the normal rappel from Dewey Peak, then decided to look for an alternative anchor.

Climber 1 selected a large block to sling for an anchor. The rock was about the size of a microwave oven and tilted only slightly above horizontal in orientation. After debating the merits of this anchor and looking for other options, the party agreed to use the large rock as the primary anchor and place a backup for the first couple of rappellers.

The primary anchor consisted of a doubled cordelette slung over the rock and tied into a master point. The backup was a cam placed in a crack four to six feet behind the cordelette anchor. The cam was connected to the cordelette by a prusik cord hitched to two opposed non-locking carabiners, which were clipped to the cordelette on top of the block.

The climbers rappelled with a doubled 60-meter rope. Climber 1 went first, based on the idea that he was the heaviest and could straighten out rope tangles ahead of the two student climbers. Climber 2 rappelled second. Climber 3 (male, age 35) was told by Climber 1 to clean the cam anchor before rappelling. He removed the cam and carabiners clipped to the top side of the cordelette anchor. As he rappelled, the cordelette slipped off the rock and Climber 3 fell to his death.

ANALYSIS

Tacoma Mountain Rescue and the National Park Service revisited the scene of the accident on August 25 and re-created the rappel anchors, based on photographs taken by Climber 3 before the accident and recovered from his phone. An evaluation determined that the two carabiners connecting the cordelette to the prusik sling had helped hold the cordelette in place. When the first two people to rappel loaded the cordelette with their weight, the carabiners essentially pinned the cordelette in place on top of the block. Once these carabiners were removed, the cordelette was only held in place by friction, which was insufficient to keep it from rolling and slipping off the rock.

As is often the case with alpine climbing accidents, this was the result of a series of decisions, any one of which might have prevented the accident. These include:

- Not using the peak's standard rappel anchor.
- Rappelling instead of downclimbing or lowering the student climbers.
- Choosing a block anchor without a sufficient lip or horn to hold the cord securely.
- Use of cord instead of slings to build the anchor (sling material would not be as prone to rolling).
- Loosely slinging the cordelette rather than girth-hitching it around the block.
- Arranging the backup in such a way that the cordelette had to be lifted to clean the carabiners, possibly making the cordelette less secure.
- Putting an inexperienced climber in the position of cleaning the backup, evaluating if the cordelette anchor had been compromised by removing the cam and carabiners, and rappelling without a backup. (*Source: Tacoma Mountain Rescue.*)

FALL ON ROCK | Broken Hold, Inadequate Protection
North Cascades, Concord Tower

Shortly before 10:30 a.m. on August 28, Benjamin G. Antonio (67) was climbing on the north side of Concord Tower, near Washington Pass, when a handhold broke and Antonio fell. He swung about 45 feet and hit the wall feet first. His partner lowered Antonio to a ledge, where a doctor who was in the area assessed his injuries. (Concord's north face is directly opposite the very popular southwest face of Liberty Bell.)

Antonio activated his personal locator beacon, and several other people in the area used their inReach devices to call for help, advising that the patient was suspected of having a possible broken pelvis and back injury. King County sent a helicopter crew, but they were unable to hoist Antonio out due to the difficult terrain. A crew from Naval Air Station Whidbey Island responded and airlifted Antonio to Seattle. (*Source: Chelan County Sheriff's Office.*)

ANALYSIS

Holds should be tested before weighting them, especially in a mountain environment. Given the long fall, the leader does not appear to have placed adequate protection. This party was prepared with an emergency device to call for help, as were others in the area, which sped the rescue. (*Source: The Editors.*)

WEST VIRGINIA

GROUND FALL | Broken Hold, Inadequate Protection
Seneca Rocks, Green Wall

On April 14, Tom H. (44) and Chris C. (35) were climbing at Seneca Rocks for their first outing of the season. It was Tom's first trip to Seneca. They started with Pleasant Overhangs (5.7) on the Green Wall, and at 7:30 a.m., after scrambling up to the belay ledge, Tom began leading the first pitch by way of a variation start. After climbing ten feet, he felt the protection was too sparse and uncertain to continue. Rather than downclimb, he decided to traverse 15 feet across an unprotected, blocky, and slightly overhanging face to gain the primary route. During the traverse, a handhold broke off and he fell 17 to 20 feet into a gap between the cliff face and a large boulder. Tom suffered a closed pilon fracture of the left ankle (tibia) and a broken right middle finger. He was wearing a helmet.

After determining that it was not possible to self-evacuate, Chris downclimbed 5th-class terrain from the belay ledge to summon additional help. Within minutes, four climbers responded, and within one hour 10 to 12 additional climbers came to assist, one of whom secured a litter from the rescue cache on the approach trail. Initial responders had limited wilderness first aid or high-angle rescue skills, which made it difficult to rig the litter for a safe lower, as the area consisted of mostly 5th-class terrain, talus, and trees. A guide with Seneca Rocks Climbing School eventually joined the rescue, and his knowledge greatly assisted the lowering process.

ANALYSIS
Tom, though an experienced climber, was unfamiliar with this crag. The better choice when deciding against the variation would have been to downclimb. Instead, the off-route traverse took him over loose, blocky rock. After two surgeries, Tom uses a prosthetic brace for mobility. (*Source: Tom H.*)

FALL ON ROCK | Loose Rock, Inadequate Protection
Seneca Rocks, Church Rocks

On October 7, Adam and Amber (both 26) were at a rock formation called Church Rocks, an infrequently climbed area near Seneca Rocks. After completing a route to the top of the formation, the climbers decided to rappel from a different location in order to scope out another wall they had noticed earlier. During the rappel, Adam identified a finger-sized crack he wanted to climb, and after cleaning some loose rock and debris, he continued to a ledge that offered a nice stance and was 25 feet off the ground. Amber then rappelled to this ledge.

Adam racked up, clipped their belay anchor as his first piece, and started up the route. At approximately ten feet above the belay, Adam encountered a large rock at the base of the crack system. He had checked this block on his initial descent and it felt, looked, and sounded solid, so he placed his first piece, a number 1 Tricam (red),

ESSENTIALS

WOUND MANAGEMENT
FROM GOBIES TO SERIOUS LACERATIONS

By R. Bryan Simon

Though often not reported, the most common injuries for climbing and other outdoor pursuits are wounds such as abrasions, lacerations, and, to a lesser extent, puncture wounds. Such injuries may come from leader falls, rockfall, attempts to self-arrest in snow, and, of course, hand jams. An understanding of wound care principles is useful for all climbers, whether dealing with a gobie after climbing a long splitter crack or stopping major bleeding after a fall.

STOP THE BLEEDING

While many injuries in the backcountry will not require this step, treatment of any major laceration or puncture wound is likely to start with direct pressure. To stop uncontrolled bleeding, place the cleanest material possible over the wound and apply pressure directly over the site with your hands for a minimum of five minutes. If possible, raise the injured area above the heart. Once the bleeding has stopped, create a pressure dressing over the wound (see below).

Many first-aid kits include hemostatic gauze or bandages (they can be purchased at outdoor retailers or pharmacies), and these can be very useful for profuse bleeding. If direct pressure is unable to stop severe bleeding, consider the use of a tourniquet and begin evacuation immediately.

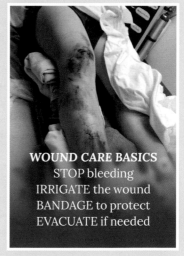

WOUND CARE BASICS
STOP bleeding
IRRIGATE the wound
BANDAGE to protect
EVACUATE if needed

Photo: Adam Happensack

CLEAN THE WOUND

This is likely the most important factor in wound care for long-term healing and prevention of infection. Irrigating the wound should be done as soon as possible, with the cleanest water available. If possible, use at least one liter of clean water and rinse the wound using pressurized flow. If a good first-aid kit is available, use a 30–60 ml syringe with an 18-gauge needle to create a spray of fluid. Field-expedient methods to apply irrigation include puncturing a corner of a clean plastic bag with a small safety pin, adding water, and squeezing the bag. (This can also be replicated by punching a small hole in a water bottle lid.) Squeezing a hydration bladder also can provide high-pressure irrigation, though the bite valve should be removed to prevent introduction of bacteria harbored in the valve.

After irrigating the wound, it may be necessary to physically remove debris from the area. Over the years, we have had a number of reports of objects impaled in climbers after falls, including ice axes, carabiners, and tree branches. If any of these items is near vital structures such as large arteries, body cavities, or the face, they should not be removed, but instead should be stabilized in place, and evacuation should begin immediately.

BANDAGE TO PROTECT

Bandaging protects a wound from further contamination and should be completed as soon as possible after irrigation. For simple wounds, use sterile gauze or the cleanest material available, such as a spare T-shirt or other extra clothing. If using a non-sterile bandage, apply antibiotic cream to the wound, as this will help prevent bacteria or other debris from coming into contact with damaged tissue.

Complex and high-risk wounds include those still open after eight hours, wounds from animal bites, puncture wounds, crush wounds with a large amount of damaged tissue, and deep wounds to the hands and feet. Care for these wounds requires you to stop the bleeding using direct pressure, copiously irrigate with potable water, dress and pack wounds with wet sterile dressings, cover the area with sterile or clean bandages, wrap the affected body part, and apply a pressure dressing if needed. Pressure dressings can be created by tightly wrapping the affected body part with whatever materials are available and tying a knot directly above the wound.

Only consider closing wounds in the backcountry, either with sutures or with Steri-Strips, if you have the required knowledge and materials; if so, monitor the wounds closely for infection.

EVACUATE IF NEEDED

Generally speaking, simple abrasions do not require evacuation unless they are located on the bottoms of the feet, the palms, or the genitalia, or if an abrasion begins to show signs of severe infection. Any lacerations that involve tendons, ligaments, or nerves, or cause severe bleeding, should be evacuated immediately. Large lacerations and puncture wounds, especially deep ones, likely require evacuation, as these are difficult to clean and are highly susceptible to infection. Additionally, any animal bites or wounds that are grossly contaminated with organic matter should be evaluated quickly by a medical professional. Tetanus and/or rabies vaccinations may be needed.

R. Bryan Simon, RN, is senior editor of ANAC and co-author of Vertical Aid: Essential Wilderness Medicine for Climbers, Trekkers, and Mountaineers.

PROTECT YOURSELF

Anytime you treat an injured climber, be aware of the risk associated with exposure to blood and body fluids (e.g. HIV, hepatitis). Carry disposable gloves (nitrile or latex) in your first-aid kit to prevent coming into contact with these fluids, and always dispose of bloody bandages and gear in a sealable container. After treatment, wash your hands with soap and water (if they are visibly bloody) or use an alcohol-based sanitizer if no blood is visible.

in a crack alongside the block. He climbed a body length higher and was reaching for a piece on his harness when his left handhold broke, causing him to fall. The Tricam held briefly, then snapped from the crack as the block pulled from the wall. Adam continued to fall past the anchor and into a small tree, which detached from the rock face and also fell. His fall came to a stop when he loaded the anchor, pulling Amber into it. The detached block hit the belayer, but she maintained her belay, catching him with her Black Diamond ATC.

Having sustained no serious injury, Adam returned to the ledge, where he clipped into the anchor and assessed Amber's wounds (bruising and puncture wounds to the right knee and a deep laceration to her right lower leg). The pair tied clean clothing around the wounds to protect them from dirt, and then, after wrestling their rope from the downed tree, Adam rigged a fixed line and they rappelled to the ground. With the help of non-climbing bystanders and members of Seneca Rocks Climbing School, they were assisted to local facilities for care. (*Source: Adam Happensack.*)

ANALYSIS

When climbing in new or seldom-visited areas, be alert for loose rock, vegetation, and insecure holds. Consider placing additional protection in these circumstances. (*Sources: Adam Happensack and the Editors.*)

FALL ON ROCK | Protection Pulled, Inadequate Protection
Seneca Rocks, Southern Pillar

In the early afternoon of November 4, a male climber (age unknown) was leading the route Climbin' Punishment (5.8+). The climber fell when he was approximately 75 feet up the route, while negotiating the second of two overhanging steps. His highest piece pulled when it was loaded, causing him to fall 25 to 30 feet before the belayer (male, age unknown) arrested the fall.

The climber was inverted during the fall and impacted a ledge with his upper back and head. He lost consciousness and was lowered to the ground, where he regained consciousness. The belayer called for assistance, and the injured climber was carried to the nearby road and then transferred by helicopter to a local medical facility. The climber suffered a fractured skull, concussion, and minor lacerations to his head and right shoulder. He was wearing a helmet, which may have saved his life.

ANALYSIS

Although the exact circumstances that caused this protection piece to pull out of the rock are not known, there are various possibilities. This climb has several hollow flakes and flaring cracks, and gear placed in hollow or loose rock can exert enough force to shift the rock and cause placements to fail. Protecting flaring cracks can be tricky as well. In such cases, doubling up on protection and/or placing pro more frequently than usual are wise precautions. In addition, protection that isn't extended adequately with a quickdraw or sling can be shifted out of its ideal placement by the movement of the rope. This is especially true when the rope changes direction, such as while negotiating roofs or traverses. (*Source: Adam Happensack, Seneca Rocks Climbing School.*)

WISCONSIN

FATAL GROUND FALL | Protection Pulled
Devil's Lake State Park, East Bluff, Pedestal Buttress

On March 28 at approximately 3:45 p.m., Savannah Buik, 22, fell while leading Birch Tree Crack, a 5.8 climb on the Pedestal Buttress. A witness said she fell approximately 20 feet from the crux of the climb to the ground, landing on her back on rocky, uneven terrain at the base of the climb. She was wearing a helmet. The witness believes she had placed two cams that pulled out during the fall, the first of which was a number 2 (yellow) Camalot that was attached to an extended alpine draw. The witness remembers her calling to the belayer that she was readjusting this piece after its initial placement.

After the fall, nearby climbers came to her immediate assistance, calling 911 and initiating CPR until emergency medical services arrived. EMS attached an AED (defibrillator), and after checking for signs of life, confirmed that she had passed away. (*Sources: Eyewitness and published reports.*)

CAMS IN SLIPPERY ROCK

Numerous reports document that well-placed cams can pull out of hard, slippery stone like the quartzite at Devil's Lake. (*The first pitch of Zodiac on El Capitan is notorious for this phenomenon—see* ANAC 2018.) What can be done to minimize this hazard?

- Lubricate cams and fix or replace units with sticky lobes or bent trigger wires.
- Avoid placements in damp or icy rock.
- Choose the right cam for a placement—it should fit in the unit's optimum camming range.
- Orient the placement in the direction of anticipated load, and extend the placement with a quickdraw or sling to maintain the correct orientation.
- Look for constrictions in the crack that will increase a cam's holding power (like a nut).
- Never say "good enough." If a placement doesn't look great, fix it or find another.
- Use more nuts: A well-placed nut may be more resistant to pulling out of slick rock than a cam.

ANALYSIS
Savannah Buik was an experienced climber and the chair of the AAC's Chicago Chapter, and this route was within her ability level. It is impossible to say why she fell or exactly why her protection pulled out of the crack, but the very hard and slick quartzite at Devil's Lake is unforgiving of imperfect protection placements (see sidebar on this page). The crux of this climb comes early, making any fall that pulls out protection very serious. Protect frequently, consider passive protection in slippery rock, and be vigilant in the placement and assessment of your gear. (*Source: The Editors.*)

WYOMING

FALL DURING DESCENT | Inexperience, Inadequate Gear
Grand Teton National Park, Symmetry Spire

On June 12, at about 9:30 p.m., rescue coordinator George Montopoli received a call about an accident in the descent gully (southwest couloir) on Symmetry Spire. The caller informed Montopoli that he and his climbing partner had left the valley at about 7 a.m. and reached the base of the southwest ridge route (5.7) at about noon, when they ate all their food. They completed the climb and rappelled to the col at the top of the couloir at about 9 p.m. Although the reporting climber had an ice axe and was able to descend the steep, hard-packed snow in the couloir, his partner had left his axe at the base of the climb and was forced to downclimb exposed rock and scree to the west of the snow. A short distance down from the col, the partner slipped and fell about 30 feet along a steep rock step. He then tumbled down rock and scree into trees that prevented him from reaching the snow and falling further. He suffered a broken right ankle and broken left fibula.

A two-member hasty team, followed by three additional rangers carrying heavier rescue and support gear, responded to the accident scene, located at an elevation of about 10,200 feet. Steep, firm snow in Symmetry Couloir (the approach to the spire) necessitated the use of ice axe and crampons for around 2,000 vertical feet. The hasty team arrived at about 1 a.m. and provided medical attention, warm clothing, shelter, and food to the two climbers, who had not packed for spending the night outdoors. The ambient air temperature was approximately 30°F. The second group of rescuers arrived at about 2:40 a.m. and continued support for the two climbers. The following morning, the two were extracted from the scene, one at a time, by helicopter short-haul. (*Source: National Park Service Search and Rescue Report.*)

ANALYSIS
The two male climbers (both 18 years old) had inadequate inexperience for such a route, and this showed in many ways: a relatively late start, a slow approach and a long time spent on the route, inadequate food and gear for a big day (including no extra gear for an unexpected night out), and the fateful decision to leave one ice axe at the base of the climb, even though a snowy descent obviously was in store. Online research and/or a preclimb chat with the rangers at Jenny Lake can provide a wealth of information—it's up to climbers to use it well. (*Source: The Editors.*)

STRANDED | Off-Route, Inadequate Preparation, Darkness
Grand Teton National Park, Teewinot Mountain

On June 16, at 11:23 p.m., Teton Interagency Dispatch Center received a call from an uninjured father (33) and son (13) in the vicinity of the southwest couloir of Teewinot, at roughly 11,000 feet. They reported leaving the trailhead that morning at 9:30 to climb the east face of Teewinot. They had carried ice axes but no crampons, one headlamp,

The east face of Teewinot (shown here) is a snow climb in early season. In June, two climbers were stranded on the southwest side after ascending this face. A fatal fall later in the month (see report below) ended in the area marked. *NPS Photo*

and one rain jacket between them. By 11 p.m., they reported, they had made six rappels down the southwest side of Teewinot, then stopped as they did not want to continue rappelling with one headlamp into unknown terrain. They were not carrying overnight gear. Light rain and lightning persisted between 11 p.m. and 1 a.m. Coordinates for the father and son were found via a 911 "ping" as well as the Gaia app on the father's smartphone.

At 2:30 a.m. on June 17, a ranger team headed up the mountain, and at 7:30 a.m. they made contact with the two individuals and began a technical snow lower into Glacier Gulch. After warming the father and son, the rangers walked everyone out to the Lupine Meadows Trailhead. (*Source: National Park Service Search and Rescue Report.*)

ANALYSIS

These two were underequipped and underprepared for a climb as significant as Teewinot in mid-June, when the east face is a moderate but long snow climb. They started much too late for such a big route (more than 5,500 vertical feet). Asked why they did not return down the east face route, the father told rangers he was not comfortable descending the terrain they had just ascended, even though they were equipped to rappel. Instead, they headed down unfamiliar technical terrain. The two made a good decision to stop when they did, as continuing down in darkness and storm, with only one headlamp and significant fatigue, might have led to a much worse outcome. (*Source: The Editors.*)

FATAL FALL ON SNOW | Failure to Control Glissade
Grand Teton National Park, Teewinot Mountain

At approximately 7:45 a.m. on June 25, an individual was reported overdue from a solo climb up the east face of Teewinot Mountain. The overdue climber, a 27-year-old male, had posted a video onto social media from the summit around 4:30 the previous afternoon. His vehicle was still at the Lupine Meadows Trailhead. Rangers started up toward the east face of Teewinot, and at approximately 11 a.m. they observed a blue object at the base of the face through a spotting scope. About 15 minutes later, the two rangers reached the location and confirmed that it was the missing climber and that he was deceased. The body was recovered by helicopter long-line.

ANALYSIS

An aerial reconnaissance of the upper east face conducted the day the body was discovered revealed that the climber had most likely tried to glissade the upper snow-field at 12,000 feet, lost control, and fell approximately 2,400 feet. Generally, climbers on a slope of this angle and exposure would choose to plunge step or downclimb in order to descend safely. The climber was dressed for a day climb with a light pack, helmet, and boots. He carried an ice axe. He was not wearing crampons, but had a pair in his pack, which would be consistent with glissading versus downclimbing. (*Source: National Park Service Search and Rescue Report.*)

ROCKFALL IN DESCENT GULLY
Grand Teton National Park, Disappointment Peak

At approximately 3:30 p.m. on June 28, an experienced climber (male, age 68) was struck by a rolling rock while scrambling down a descent gully after a climb of the Open Book (5.9+), a popular multi-pitch route above Garnet Canyon. The rock hit the climber's lower left leg, and the resulting laceration and contusion prevented him from walking. With his partner's help, he was able to "crab" his way down to the Garnet Canyon Trail.

Rangers reached the pair a little after 6 p.m., and after assessing the injured climber and discussing options for evacuation, a helicopter extraction was deemed prudent and appropriate. The injured climber was extracted via short-haul and flown to Lupine Meadows. His partner hiked out and drove him to the hospital for further evaluation and treatment. (*Source: National Park Service Search and Rescue Report.*)

ANALYSIS
Accidents involving rockfall or rolling rocks in descent gullies are not uncommon. General advice for minimizing the hazard in loose terrain includes: Stay close together while descending; descend one at a time through loose passages or "chokes" in gullies, while other members of the party wait in a safe zone; communicate with your partners when negotiating a loose section and yell "Rock!" if anything comes off; and wear your helmet. An alternative descent from this popular climb, with minimal scrambling, heads east to reach Amphitheater Lake and a hiking trail. (*Source: The Editors.*)

RAPPEL ERROR | Device Installed Incorrectly
Grand Teton National Park, Cascade Canyon, Storm Point

At approximately 10:30 p.m. on July 22, Teton Interagency Dispatch Center received a call from a hiker who stated he was hiking east on the Cascade Canyon Trail when he heard calls for help and saw lights flashing on the cliffs above the trail. Rangers Fletcher and Edmonds headed up Cascade Canyon to attempt to make contact with the party in distress. They were able to observe light flashing about three pitches up the Guide's Wall climbing route (5.8 to 5.10c, depending on variations).

Edmonds and Fletcher were unable to access the subject due to the darkness and lack of technical climbing equipment on hand, but were able to confirm that a female climber was alone, uninjured, and without a rope partway up the route. At 4 a.m., rangers Kreis and Ronczkowski departed the rescue cache with climbing equipment, arriving at the base of Guide's Wall at approximately 5:15 a.m. Kreis and Ronczkowski then proceeded to climb several pitches to reach the stranded climber.

The rangers made contact with the subject at 6:30 a.m. She stated that her climbing partner had fallen while rappelling, along with their only rope, the previous evening. The rangers could see the partner, motionless, approximately 300 feet below their location. They assisted the stranded climber down the wall.

The fallen partner (male, age 33) was deceased. A long-line helicopter recovery mission was conducted later that day.

ANALYSIS

The two climbers were attempting to descend from Guide's Wall by rappelling using a single 70-meter rope, although rappelling with two ropes is standard on this route. The two arrived at an intermediate rappel station on a small ledge about 20 to 30 feet above a large ledge at the bottom of what is usually the first rappel.

The first climber, according to his partner, then set up a short rappel, only feeding about 30 to 40 feet of rope through the anchor, judging this to be sufficient to reach the ledge just below. He put on a puffy jacket immediately before setting up

Reconstruction of the rappel setup found on a climber who fell at Guide's Wall. It's believed the climber wrapped the autoblock around both strands of his rappel rope, but he failed to insert one strand of rope through the rappel device and clip it into his carabiner. As soon as he weighted the system, the unclipped strand pulled right through the autoblock backup. *NPS Photo*

his rappel device. The partner states that she was looking away when she heard him say "Whoops" in a distinctly casual manner, at which she looked in his direction and saw him falling. After realizing her partner had fallen with the rope, she was able to use a series of shoulder-length slings to down-aid to the ledge, where she yelled for help and attracted the attention of passing hikers.

Rangers were able to inspect the anchor from which the climber had fallen and rule out anchor failure as a cause of the accident.

The climber was found rigged for rappel with a Black Diamond ATC Guide and an autoblock (i.e., a "third hand") backup, each clipped to his harness with independent locking carabiners. A single strand of the climbing rope passed through the ATC and locking carabiner, which was attached to the harness belay loop. The autoblock, clipped to a harness leg loop, was wrapped around the single strand of rope as it exited the ATC with approximately 190 to 200 feet of rope beyond it. The autoblock was not wrapped around the 30 to 40 feet of climbing rope leading out of the ATC in the opposite direction.

Based on interviews with the partner and the evidence found at the scene, investigators concluded the primary cause of this accident appeared to be a rappel rigging error. The climber appears to have only clipped one of the two strands of rappel rope when attaching his ATC. He was an experienced climber and would not have committed this error out of ignorance. The partner's statement that she had just given him a puffy coat, which he subsequently put on, suggests that perhaps this coat concealed this error. It is likely that a bight of rope was pushed into the ATC but was not captured with the locking carabiner, yet gave the appearance of being properly clipped. Once he committed his body weight over the edge, the bight of rope would have instantly popped out of the ATC.

It may be in this moment that the subject uttered "Whoops," as he would have expected the autoblock backup that he had installed on both ropes to hold him. However, repeated tests during the investigation showed that an autoblock *does not* hold in this scenario. When only one of the strands of the rappel rope is correctly inserted into the device and clipped to the climber's harness, the climber's weight on that strand will cause the other strand (not clipped correctly) to move upward, toward the anchor. The autoblock will not hold when only one strand is through the rappel device and the two strands are moving in opposite directions. (*Source: National Park Service Search and Rescue Report.*)

Editor's note: No climbing system, including a friction-hitch backup, is completely foolproof. Once your rappel setup is completed, weight-testing the system before unclipping your tether from the anchor will verify your setup is correct.

BENIGHTED | Inexperience
Grand Teton National Park, Grand Teton

On August 2, at approximately 8:25 p.m., rangers were notified that a party was uninjured but lost on the Petzoldt Ridge of the Grand Teton and needed help. Cell phone reception was poor, but a ranger was able to communicate with the party via text message. The party was comprised of four young men, and they had just completed the rappel from the top of the Petzoldt Ridge. They were concerned about their ability to survive the night due to high winds and cold temperatures.

The ranger explained that help could not arrive until morning and gave them information on the most sheltered location to spend the night. He also provided encouragement and tips on how to survive an unplanned bivouac. Due to low battery power on their cell phone, they were advised to turn it off until morning.

At 6 a.m. rangers attempted to text and call the party multiple times without success. A ranger started up Garnet Canyon in an attempt to intercept the party, in case they had decided to carry on throughout the night. Additionally, two Exum Mountain Guides who were on the Grand Teton were advised of the situation.

At 12:15 p.m., Exum guide Zahan Billimoria encountered the group high on the Upper Exum Ridge, moving slowly toward the summit. Billimoria assisted them to the top and down the Owen Spalding descent route to below the Upper Saddle. A ranger arrived on scene at 2 p.m. and escorted the party below the Lower Saddle, where it was determined they were capable of completing the hike to the trailhead without further assistance. (*Source: National Park Service Search and Rescue Report.*)

ANALYSIS
First-timers on the Grand Teton often are surprised by the scale of the climb and the difficulty of route-finding, which is why it's wise to do your first climb of the Grand with a guide or experienced mentor.

Carrying adequate clothing, food, and emergency shelter for an unexpected night out is essential on alpine routes. Note the word "adequate"—it is not practical to load packs with enough gear to ensure a comfortable night and still make it up a long technical climb. Pack an ultralight waterproof tarp (such as a siltarp), extra layers, and some extra food, get out of the wind, and huddle for warmth—if a party can stay dry and fed, the night may be miserable but it will not be life-threatening.

Mobile phones are increasingly useful tools for mountain navigation and communication—in certain areas—but a cold night will rapidly drain a phone's battery. Keep the phone warm (inside your clothing), resist the temptation to turn it on for non-essential reasons, and consider carrying an extra battery pack. Rewarming a "dead" phone can sometimes restore limited service. (*Source: The Editors.*)

STRANDED | Unable to Retrieve Rappel Rope
Wind River Range, Cirque of the Towers, Wolf's Head Peak

At approximately midnight on September 1, Sublette County Sheriff's Office dispatch received a call from a couple of climbers (male and female) who were stranded on the northwest face of Wolf's Head, not far below the summit. Their rappel rope had become stuck during their descent, after climbing the classic east ridge. The climbers reported they had supplies to spend the night on the three-foot ledge they were on, but would need assistance in the morning.

At first light on September 2, Tip Top Search and Rescue helicoptered to the area with a short-haul team, and the crew dropped an additional rappel rope, a team radio, water, and extra food to the climbers, as the stranded male was a Type 1 diabetic. The two felt they were in good enough condition to self-evacuate with the supplies given. Tip Top's short-haul team landed in a nearby meadow to monitor the descent in case they needed further assistance.

Over the next couple of hours, the two became disoriented and struggled to continue. They had lost a bag with personal gear and medical supplies required for the male's diabetes. His medical condition was beginning to worsen, and his climbing partner was able to communicate the change in status with the awaiting search and rescue team. The short-haul team rigged the helicopter, and despite high, swirling winds on the cliff face, successfully brought both members off the mountain to the meadow below. The helicopter subsequently flew all parties out of the mountains. (*Source: Sublette County Sheriff's Office.*)

ANALYSIS

This is a good example of the "snowball effect" that can compound the seriousness of relatively small problems. It's not known when the party reached the summit, but darkness and fatigue undoubtedly contributed to their stranding. Before attempting remote alpine routes, it's essential to acquire the skills and carry the equipment to recover a stuck rope, either by ascending the rope or by climbing back to the rappel anchor. Since they were unable to do either, they were forced to spend the night at around 12,000 feet, which contributed to the need for a helicopter rescue in the morning.

Note that these climbers and at least one previous party on Wolf's Head were able to contact authorities in Pinedale by mobile phone. However, this should be considered a rare anomaly—there is no reliable cell service in most parts of these mountains. (*Source: The Editors.*)

FALL ON ROCK | Off-Route, Inadequate Protection
Vedauwoo, Nautilus

It always starts out like a casual day. Perfect weather, great friends, no need to push yourself. The next thing you know you're sitting on your couch in a cast and writing an accident report for ANAC.

I work for the American Alpine Club, and we were on a staff outing to Vedauwoo in early June. For the second climb of the day, I suggested to my co-worker Craig that we do a two-pitch 5.6 chimney called H&H Grunt, which would be nice and cool inside, while we waited for harder climbs to come into the shade. Craig led the first pitch, and I took the lead for the second pitch, burrowing through a vertical tunnel. It was fun and well protected until I pulled onto a ledge where I was faced with about 15 feet of unprotected face and crystal climbing to get to a bolted anchor.

I could tell I was no longer on what I considered to be 5.6 terrain, but Vedauwoo is known for sandbags and runouts. I downclimbed to see if I had missed something, but every option looked more difficult. Back on the ledge, I looked down at my last piece of protection. It was a bomber number 4 cam, but the piece was below my feet, plus I had put a long sling on it to avoid rope drag. About six feet below that piece was another ledge. I yelled down to Craig, "This looks like a bad place to fall!"

I felt confident I could make what looked to be a few 5.9 moves and then scurry to the top on easier ground. I stepped gingerly onto a couple of crystals, and almost immediately a foothold popped off. When I hit the ledge I could feel pain shoot through my right ankle. My gear had not absorbed any of the impact, although it kept me from rolling off the lower ledge. I caught my breath and took inventory: no heavy bleeding, no bones sticking out of my skin. Craig gently lowered me to the ground, and with some scooching on my butt and limping with my arms on my friends' shoulders, I was able to get to the car. A two-hour ride home got me to my couch.

After receiving X-rays and limping around on a supposed sprained ankle for four weeks, the doctor ordered an MRI and a date with an orthopedic surgeon, who said I actually had a talus fracture in my right ankle and needed surgery.

ANALYSIS
I had done the 5.6 route a few years earlier and thought I remembered using the bolted anchor above the blank slab. After the accident I reviewed the guidebook: It says to follow the chimney to a notch and then traverse right to a different set of anchors. Two co-workers who finished the route the way I tried to go to retrieve our gear said it was at least 5.9. I had been very set on where I thought the route went, and I felt I could do the moves, so I ignored some obvious warning signs.

When I was standing on the top ledge I noticed a crack at my feet. Gear placed here still would have been below my feet when I fell, but that extra piece would have shortened my fall by about three feet. If you are facing a dangerous runout, place the highest gear you can. (*Source: Carol Kotchek.*)

CANADA

Unless otherwise noted, the narratives in the Canada section are drawn from national and regional park reports. Analysis was provided by park rangers, Robert Chisnall of the Alpine Club of Canada, the Association of Canadian Mountain Guides (ACMG), and the Editors.

STRANDED | Exhaustion, Climbing Alone
Yukon Territory, Kluane National Park and Reserve, Mt. Logan

In the early morning of June 1, Parks Canada was notified that a solo climber was requesting assistance high on Mt. Logan. The climber had summited the mountain and was located at Prospector's Col, at approximately 5,500 meters. The climber was experiencing fatigue, having trouble route-finding, and getting low on food and fuel. Although a helicopter is not able to land safely at this location, a Visitor Safety team was able to drop food and supplies for the climber by air later that day.

On the afternoon of June 2, a father and son climbing team that was at Camp 4, at 5,200 meters, climbed to Prospector's Col and assisted the individual down to Camp 4. That evening, weather conditions allowed for a successful rescue of the climber at Camp 4 using a helicopter sling rescue system deployed by the Visitor Safety team and the on-site climbers.

ANALYSIS

The climbers who assisted the individual in distress were key to the success of this rescue in several ways: 1) a helicopter could not safely land at the climber's location; 2) deploying a rescue team by ground would have required additional time for acclimatization; and 3) the climber required assistance at the site to deploy the sling rescue system. In the absence of aid from these climbers, alternate rescue options would have been employed by the Visitor Safety team, but the result likely would have been an increase in complexity and duration of the operation. This incident highlights the increased risk that is associated with solo climbing.

AVALANCHE | Poor Position, Weather
British Columbia, Mt. Robson Provincial Park, Whitehorn Mountain

In the early hours of April 23, a party of two climbers from Europe left their high camp, located in the northeast bowl of Whitehorn Mountain (3,399 meters), to attempt the northeast face of the mountain. This is not believed to be an established route.

The party roped up for three pitches of waterfall ice interspersed with broad snow ledges. As the leader was approaching the top of the third ice pitch, they were struck by an avalanche. From the description and site inspection, it is suspected this was a solar-triggered soft slab avalanche of size 1.5 (on the Canadian scale that runs to size 5). The party reported that small avalanches had been coming down as soon as the sun started to shine on the face above them, and that they had nearly made it to the relative safety of the left side of the snow ledge when they were struck by the larger slide.

The party was swept down the climb and ended up in the middle of the run-out zone (2,400 meters). Both climbers ended up on the surface but were injured and unable to move. They used a satellite phone to contact a friend in Europe. From there the call went to their federal government, who contacted their embassy in Ottawa. The embassy then contacted Emergency Management British Columbia (EMBC), who notified the local SAR group (Robson Valley SAR). Robson Valley SAR requested the assistance of Parks Canada Visitor Safety staff, who conducted the rescue.

Location of the fallen climbers after an avalanche on Whitehorn Mountain. The two were most of the way up the prominent rock band directly above the debris fan when the avalanche swept them off. *Parks Canada*

ANALYSIS

The northeast face of Whitehorn Mountain was still holding winter snowpack at the time of this incident. As a result the route was exposed to a significant objective hazard from the large snow slope and cornice running the length of the ridge above the route. Despite the party getting an early start, the snow slope and the corniced ridge were catching the early morning sun. This was also the start of the first significant warming trend of the season. The party reported that they had not been able to see the significant avalanche terrain above the roped pitches from the base of the route. These climbers were not equipped with avalanche rescue gear (transceiver, probes, and shovels) and were fortunate that they ended up on the surface of the snow.

While the climbers did have a means of calling for help (which likely saved their lives), they did not have the phone numbers of the local response agencies. This delayed the response time. Had this incident occurred a few hours later in the day, the communication delay may have forced the seriously injured climbers to spend a night on the mountain.

RAPPEL ERROR | Loss of Control and Pendulum
British Columbia, Mt. Assiniboine

On July 29 a climber was descending the northeast ridge of Assiniboine and was rappelling diagonally to reach a ledge when the climber slipped and swung back into the fall line, impacting a protruding rock. The resulting injury prevented the party from continuing down the mountain. They activated a personal locator beacon (PLB). When there was no emergency response after two hours, one of the party continued descending to the Hind Hut and used the emergency radio there to call the Assiniboine Lodge for help. A Parks Canada Visitor Safety team was dispatched, and the patient was heli-slung down to the Hind Hut.

The initial PLB signal had provided coordinates that were seven kilometers south of the party's location. This caused a delay of several hours in emergency response.

ANALYSIS

Even a modest swing on rappel can cause serious injuries, and this accident reinforces the importance of rappelling with a "third hand" backup, in case a person is incapacitated or loses control because of an incident during a rappel. Why the PLB coordinates were inaccurate is unclear. It is possible the device was being switched on and off and thus did not obtain and send more accurate coordinates, or the party's location on the mountain may have been suboptimal for the PLB to communicate with satellites. Make sure the emergency contact associated with your communication device is up to date and that the contact knows your climbing plans; this can help immensely in the case of a confusing emergency signal. It is also recommended that parties traveling in the mountains carry a two-way emergency communication device, in order to provide immediate updates and location confirmation.

The Silverhorn route on Mt. Athabasca generally follows the left skyline of the foreground subpeak. An early season slab avalanche carried two climbers 600 meters down the route. *ACMG Photo*

AVALANCHE
Alberta, Mt. Athabasca

At around 10:30 a.m. on September 19, two climbers triggered an avalanche on the Silverhorn route. The weather was clear, with light winds, and the temperature was near 0° Celsius. The leader described the snow as being "Styrofoam-like." They had seen no signs of instability. The team was at an altitude of 3,200 meters, about 200 meters below the top, on a northern aspect, when the avalanche occurred. The party heard and felt a "whumph" underfoot, and an avalanche swept the roped pair down the mountain for 600 meters before they came to a stop.

One member was partially buried, with head and one arm exposed. Both climbers were carrying shovels, probes, and beacons, and the partner was able to excavate the partially buried climber. ACMG guides witnessed the avalanche, reported it, and assisted the two climbers. The team was transported by helicopter to Jasper, where one of the climbers was diagnosed with a fractured ankle.

ANALYSIS
Moderate winds and warming temperatures had created consolidated wind slabs over older faceted snow lying on ice. The top of this face transitions from 50° to 25° slopes, and the slab on this broad convexity was thinner and more prone to collapse. The avalanche was estimated to measure 500 meters by 750 meters and 0.4 meters thick (size 2.5). The team was prepared with the appropriate emergency equipment.

AVALANCHE | Poor Position
Alberta, David Thompson Highway, Elliot Peak

Four climbers were involved in an avalanche incident below the Kitty Hawk ice climb (3 pitches, WI5) on the east side of Elliot Peak. An avalanche swept down the route just after one of the climbers had rappelled off Unicorn, a short M7 mixed route that begins just to the left of Kitty Hawk. This climber had serious but non-life-threatening injuries. The four activated an emergency locator beacon just after noon and then managed to self-evacuate to the highway, where they met responders. The injured climber was flown to a hospital in Edmonton.

ANALYSIS
This ice climb is well-known to have very serious avalanche hazard in certain conditions. The avalanche danger at the time in this general area was rated moderate to considerable for subalpine terrain. (*Sources: Published reports and the Editors.*)

FALLING TREE | Situational Awareness
Alberta, Lake Louise, Back of the Lake

On June 13, a tree fell from above the Outhouse Wall at the Back of the Lake area and struck three climbers who were at the base. One climber (male, age 26) was flown to a hospital by air ambulance and later died from his injuries. A second climber was transported to Banff Mineral Springs Hospital with moderate injuries, and a third was able to walk out from the area without assistance.

ANALYSIS
The cliffs at Back of the Lake line the foot of a steep mountain that extends far above the climbing areas. The tree or part of a tree that hit the climbers is believed to have fallen 80 to 100 meters and may have been toppled by high wind. A reconnaissance flight after the incident suggested there were dozens of dead trees above these popular cliffs.

It was reported that the climber who later died (male, mid-20s) was not wearing a helmet when the tree fell, while the other two climbers were wearing helmets. This is a stark reminder that helmets should be donned as soon as climbers enter an area with significant overhead hazard—don't wait until the rope is flaked out. Considering the known risk at this area, climbers might consider another destination when high wind is forecast. (*Source: ACMG report, other published reports, and the Editors.*)

FATAL FALL ON ICE | Climbing Alone, Weather
Alberta, Banff National Park, Cascade Falls

On Christmas day, a male climber, 26, fell a significant distance while soloing frozen Cascade Falls and died as a result of his injuries. Cascade Falls is a very popular ice route (300m, WI3) near the town of Banff.

ANALYSIS
The dangers of unroped soloing are obvious. The temperature on this day was well above freezing, with recent intermittent rain. The ice may have been in poor condition. There have been previous accidents (including at least one fatality) on this route as a result of rockfall and avalanches. (*Sources: Published accounts and the Editors.*)

ICE CLIMBING GROUND FALL | Rapidly Changing Conditions
Alberta, Banff National Park, Mt. Wilson

On Monday, March 12, an experienced party had decided to climb the route Ice Nine on Mt. Wilson. This is a 90-meter, WI6 route that had been seeing frequent ascents and was described as being in "WI5" shape. The weather was clear, with cold overnight temperatures and warm days, resulting in increasing avalanche danger throughout the day. The party had started early to take advantage of the cold weather and low avalanche danger in the morning and to be out of the area before conditions deteriorated.

At around 7 a.m., the leader started up the first pitch. When he was about four meters up, his tool sheared through some chandelier ice and he fell to the ground. He landed on his feet, but complained of back pain and other concerns. The party had a radio, so they called Parks Canada for help.

Two Parks Canada rescue specialists responded via helicopter from Banff. They slung onto the site, immobilized the injured climber, and slung him to a waiting ambulance. The climber was transported by ambulance to Banff, where it was confirmed that he had several stable spinal compressions. The full injuries were not discovered until later with an MRI: He ended up having four stable compression breaks in his lower back and a cracked pelvis. They did not require surgery.

Left: Accident site below the Ice Nine ice route on Mt. Wilson. The patient fell to the ground when a tool sheared through chandelier ice. *Parks Canada* Right: Rescuer arriving by helicopter at the accident scene. *Bob O'Rourke*

ANALYSIS

Waterfall ice is a dynamic medium, and climbing it safely requires experience, skill, and attention to changing conditions. The danger can be minimized, but there will always be a certain level of risk accepted by waterfall ice climbers. The injured climber wrote an in-depth analysis of the decision-making factors influencing this incident:

(1) *Fatigue.* He had a poor sleep the night before and an early morning start. It was the end of a long trip, and he was going home in a few days, so his mind was on other things.

(2) *Familiarity.* He had climbed Ice Nine a few times earlier that season, and it was in good shape. He felt it would be a relatively easy day.

(3) *Peer pressure.* Some friends had come up right behind them. The injured climber didn't feel overly pressured but stated that he likely rushed more than normal.

(4) *Not adapting to changing conditions.* The climb had freshly formed chandelier ice on the surface. The leader had already downclimbed the first five meters once, due to the conditions, and was checking out a new line when he fell. In his words: "About ten to 15 [feet] off the ground I started to slow down and consider my options again. I didn't like it, but it did look okay higher up. As I was pondering my options, one of my tools sheared and I pitched. It was too low to have gear in, and the ice was horrible anyway. My mistake was not in the protection system but rather my inability to slow down and climb more carefully. Conditions had changed rapidly."

From a rescuer's perspective, this party did many things that made the rescue quick and safe:

(1) The party had a VHF radio programmed with the Parks Canada frequencies so they could talk directly to emergency dispatchers. This allowed the rescue specialists to accurately gauge the severity of the situation, determine what resources would be required, and pass instructions to the injured climbers. Parks Canada encourages backcountry users who will be out of cell range to carry a properly programmed VHF radio, a satellite phone, or two-way satellite texting devices for emergency communications.

(2) The party had started early and had their accident early in the day. This allowed rescuers to perform the rescue before avalanche danger rose in the afternoon.

(3) The party moved the injured climber to a spot with decreased overhead danger from ice daggers, and they chopped out a platform to help with immobilization. This sped up the patient packaging once rescuers arrived.

ROCKFALL
Alberta, Bow Valley, Heart Mountain

On August 30, a party of two was climbing Heart Line, a very long, moderate (5.9 A0) rock route in the Bow Valley. As the second climber (male, 30s) was finishing pitch four, a large boulder rolled down the climb and struck the climber in the shin, causing an open lower leg fracture. The belayer was able to lower the second to the lower belay station and then descend to the lower stance. The pair phoned 911 and a rescue was initiated. Rescuers were able to heli-sling the patient directly from the climb.

ANALYSIS

These experienced climbers were unlucky to be in the wrong location when the boulder dislodged. It is important to note they were well prepared for emergencies. They had a phone and were able to call out for help. As well, they had the skills to partially self-rescue to the lower station, thus making the ensuing rescue much easier. Both climbers had helmets and were generally well equipped.

FATAL LEADER FALL ON ROCK | Rope Cut
Alberta, Bow Valley, Yamnuska

On July 29, a party of two experienced climbers was climbing Chockstone Corner on Yamnuska's big limestone face. It is a nine-pitch climb (5.8) requiring traditional protection. The leader had started up pitch seven, about 60 meters below the top of the face. He clipped a fixed piton and placed one additional piece. After struggling with a difficult passage he fell, and the belayer watched as the climber fell past him and toward the ground far below. The belayer never felt the force of the fall on his belay device, suggesting the rope was somehow cut in the early stages of the fall. Afterward, the belayer could see the frayed end of the cut rope above him, looped over a bulge just past the fixed piton.

The belayer was stranded at the belay and called 911 with a cell phone. Rescue crews flew to the scene and confirmed the fatality. Crews then were flown to the top of the cliff. They lowered a rescuer to the stranded climber, and the rescuer and climber descended to the ground in a continuous 250-meter lower. They were then heli-slung to the staging area below.

ANALYSIS

A rope under tension can cut quite easily if it slides over a sharp or rough edge or is hit by rockfall. Yet climbing ropes very rarely fail in leader falls. What was different this time?

These climbers were experienced and certainly capable of climbing their chosen route. As with many routes on Yamnuska, Chockstone Corner involves lots of traversing. In an interview with *Gripped* magazine some time after the accident, the belayer said the leader appeared to get off-route soon after leaving the belay ledge to start the seventh pitch. "He had followed a good groove leading to a piton above the belay instead of the obvious crack on the right. He continued up right on a less-than-featured wall, aiming for easier ground above instead of going direct into the wide chimney. … At the time of the accident, the climbing was on good rock, traversing rightward across a ledge with what looked to be large boulders or blocks."

Above this ledge, the leader placed a number 2 cam, began to move again, and then returned to the cam to extend a sling to reduce rope drag. It was later learned that this cam pulled out during the fall (it was found on the ground). The belayer believes the leader was no more than five meters past the cam when he fell. On this traversing pitch, the leader's fall must have dragged the rope in such a way—perhaps around or over the blocks above the ledge—that the rope was cut before any load came onto the belayer. It's likely that when the cam pulled out, this contributed to the length and possibly the swinging nature of the fall.

The climbers were using a single "like new" 9.2mm rope. It is possible—but by no means certain—that a larger-diameter rope might have survived the fall. Leading with two half-ropes might have been a better choice, because it's unlikely that both ropes would have impacted whatever piece of rock cut the single rope, in exactly the same way, particularly if they were clipped to alternating pieces of protection, as half-ropes are supposed to be used. It's also important to consider how to keep the rope running as straight as possible—and away from edges, blocks, or notches—using protection, extension, and occasional backcleaning, as necessary. (*Sources: Alberta Parks Public Safety, Gripped, and the Editors.*)

LEADER FALL ON ROCK | Off-Route, Insufficient Protection
Alberta, Bow Valley, Goat Mountain

A party of two attempted Coire Dubh Intégral (500m, 5.7 WI3) on Goat Mountain on November 16. This is a multi-pitch ice route that leads to an upper face climbed mostly on rock and snow. The pair had left early in the day but took longer than expected. At about 6 p.m. they found themselves 100 meters from the top. Route-finding is notoriously difficult in this area, and the pair chose a finish to the right of the regular finish. As the leader was starting the final rock pitch, the climber fell. There was no protection placed at that point, so the climber hit a large sloping ledge and then tumbled past the belayer down a gully. The climber was unconscious after the fall and had serious injuries (unspecified in the report).

The partner immediately called 911 with a cell phone to request a rescue. Crews attempted to reach the pair from above that night, but high winds and fresh snow prevented a rescue. The two thus spent the night huddled on a ledge in -20°C to -15°C weather. At first light, a helicopter and crew flew to the scene and were able to heli-sling the climbers off the route to a waiting ambulance.

ANALYSIS
The climbers were fairly new to alpine climbing and as a result were moving slower than expected. They were traveling light, but they did have a couple of down jackets and some winter clothing. A shelter of some sort (such as a tarp) to retain some warmth would have helped significantly. Despite the cold night, both climbers were only mildly hypothermic.

FALL ON ROCK | Scrambling, Loose Rock, Climbing Alone
Alberta, Kananaskis Country, Mt. Smuts

On Sunday, August 12, a 27-year-old male climber was attempting a scrambling route on Mt. Smuts (2,938 meters). He did not check in that evening, and on August 13 his lifeless body was discovered by Kananaskis Emergency Services at the base of a 300-meter cliff. It appeared to first responders that he had stepped on some loose rock and fallen.

ANALYSIS

This climber was an experienced scrambler. The exact circumstances of his fall are unknown, but the standard south ridge route on Mt. Smuts is considered one of the Canadian Rockies' most difficult scrambling routes—that is, a route that is often done without a rope (though many choose to use a rope). This route likely would be graded low fifth-class. Decisions made in the mountains regarding when to scramble and when to rope up are governed by many factors, including the party's competence and experience, the quality of the rock, the weather, and the availability of protection for roped climbing. In this case, the climber was alone, so his options were limited. (*Sources: Published reports and the Editors.*)

RAPPEL ANCHOR FAILURE | Off-Route on Descent
Alberta, Waterton Lakes National Park, Sofa Mountain

Two Southern Alberta Alpine Club of Canada members climbed the snow gully route on Sofa Mountain's east face on March 13. They arrived at the summit at 3:47 p.m. and rested there, taking advantage of the warm, stable weather before descending.

At 4 p.m. they started to descend the summit ridge with the intention of traveling the normal descent route, the northeast shoulder to the summer trail. Upon leaving the summit ridge, they began scrambling down the upper cliff band on the north face. Once down, both members descended the fall line, where they began to veer off course from the normal descent route.

The two scrambled down 175 meters before reaching the first of a series of ledges on the lower cliff band. At this point they decided to follow the upper ledge west, thinking it would lead them to an easier passage to the basin below. After 150 meters they reached a steep chimney feature that was flowing with meltwater from the snowy slopes above. They decided to rappel to the lower ledge to circumvent the chimney and the water-filled channel, then continued scrambling down several ledges before reaching another dead end, approximately 20 meters above talus slopes.

With the end of their descent in sight, and with low energy levels after a long, strenuous day, team dynamics started to deteriorate as the crew split up to investigate different options. The trip leader remained on the ledge to seek a suitable rappel anchor while his partner looked for a downclimb. Eventually the partner found a steep ramp that appeared to lead to lower ledges. She shouted to inform the trip leader about her plan and began scrambling down before confirming if the leader had heard her. Suddenly she heard a loud scream from the leader, who had begun rappelling. She saw the leader fall about 10 meters from the upper ledge, land on the lower ledge, then roll off and fall another six meters to the talus; he then cartwheeled 70 or 80 meters down that steep slope. The partner climbed down to the leader, who at first appeared to be unresponsive and not breathing. Shortly after she reached him, he regained consciousness. At this point she called 911 using her cell phone.

A rescue team was deployed at 6:55 p.m., ten minutes after the accident occurred. At approximately 8:30 p.m., a medical helicopter arrived on scene, followed shortly thereafter by a rescue helicopter. Parks Canada safety technicians were dropped off by the rescue helicopter at the bottom of the basin and they hiked up to the climbers. After first aid, the patient was immobilized in a boost bag and slung down to the air ambulance waiting in the basin. The leader sustained four fractured vertebrae, other fractures, and multiple lacerations and contusions to his head and legs. He was expected to make a full recovery.

ANALYSIS

The climber had no recollection of the fall or the events leading up to the accident, so the exact cause of the accident will remain uncertain. There was no damage to the rope or cordelette (anchor), which came down with the leader, and all knots remained tight and properly dressed. It is assumed that the

Air ambulance below Sofa Mountain, awaiting a patient who fell to the marked spot in the talus from the cliffs above after his rappel anchor failed. *Parks Canada*

subject slung the cordelette around a boulder or piece of bedrock, and that the cordelette rolled off the anchor or the anchor rock shifted or became dislodged. The leader believes he might have slipped or stumbled as he started his rappel, which may have added force to the anchor.

The leader's fall easily could have been fatal. He was wearing a climbing helmet and a backpack full of gear, which protected his head, neck, and spine on impact. The helmet sustained significant damage on the back side, where the subject's head impacted the rock.

The accident occurred late in the day, and the situation easily could have led to an overnight wait for help. Fortunately, the group was in an area with cell service, which resulted in an immediate response from rescue services in Waterton and the surrounding area. The subject's climbing partner was instrumental in the rescue. Her quick thinking and first aid kept the subject stabilized until rescue crews arrived on scene. (*Sources: Parks Canada and Alpine Club of Canada blog.*)

LEADER FALL ON MIXED CLIMB | Poor Protection
Ontario, Orient Bay

I was ice climbing with two partners in the Orient Bay corridor near Nipigon over a long weekend in March. My accident occurred on the second "pitch" on what appears to be an unnamed mixed dihedral to the right of the Right Stuff in the Amy R area. One partner led a short ice ramp up to a fairly large ledge. We switched leads and I started up the somewhat chossy dihedral. I placed two cams down low and off to the side (maybe four to six feet above the belay) to keep me from falling all the way to the ground should something happen. The first real protection possibility on the route appeared to be a horizontal crack about 15 feet up. I never made it. I found a (seemingly) solid right tool placement in a crack and then tested a left hand-

Just before the fall. *Margaret Tu*

hold at about the same elevation. The rock failed my test pull, dislodged, and also released a bit of debris that was retaining my right tool placement. I fell and hit the base of the corner, slightly higher than the belay, and broke my right ankle on impact. I eventually slid down and stopped pretty much right next to my partners.

One partner called 911, and while she was on the phone, I figured out that I also had broken my right wrist, because it stopped functioning while I was untying my ropes. My partners lowered me to the ground to wait for a rescue. A local doctor was climbing nearby and heard the sirens, and this doc, bless his heart, carried a syringe of morphine in his first-aid kit, which made the wait much more pleasant. Through some rigging and brute force, the rescuers extracted me from the scene. At the hospital in Nipigon, they reset my ankle dislocation, and then I was transferred by ambulance to Thunder Bay and admitted for surgery in the wee hours of March 12. Since then I've had several more surgeries on my right ankle and right wrist, and unfortunately I've learned I have early onset arthritis and will walk with a limp.

ANALYSIS

The two pieces I placed above the ledge were only slightly higher and off to the side of the belay. There wasn't much opportunity for good gear up to the point where I fell. Attempting this somewhat chossy pitch probably wasn't the smartest choice to begin with. Many of the locations where I've ice and mixed climbed are complete junk for rock climbing, but once everything freezes in place you just climb away. In short, it was a bit of an error in judgment and probably a bit of bad luck and just some of the inherent dangers of participating in this sport. (*Source: Jason Cook.*)

MEXICO

VERY LONG FALL ONTO LEDGE | Ropes Cut by Rockfall

Nuevo León, El Potrero Chico

In December my two best friends and I were in the multi-pitch sport climbing paradise that is El Potrero Chico. It was our fourth visit to this crazy place, and we had our eyes on a 15-pitch climb called Devotion (5.11), which is notorious for being a bit run-out, hard for the grade, and chossy. We very well might have been the only people to attempt it since we'd bailed on the 10th pitch about a year earlier.

We climbed with the leader using two single ropes, being belayed on only one rope but clipping both to the bolts to avoid confusion, since the ropes looked very similar. Cruising and climbing at a steady pace, we passed the lower crux and made it to the 3rd-class seventh pitch. We had experienced some rope drag on the way up due to the system we were using, but it didn't seem too bad.

At this point I tried to link pitches eight (5.11a) and nine (5.11c), as had been recommended. So far, I hadn't taken a fall. After the first few bolts, I found myself climbing a really thin and technical slab—way too difficult for 5.11a—and inevitably I fell. I quickly realized the correct beta was to climb through a dirty, cactus-filled crack system about five feet to the right of the bolt line. I finished up pitch eight and was a couple of bolts up on pitch nine when I ran into the same problem, on an impossible slab, except this time I had a crazy amount of rope drag. There was a dihedral with plenty of holds around a corner and about five feet to the right of the bolt line. I wasn't stoked to climb with my ropes around a sharp corner, and to be extra safe, I asked my partners to belay me with both ropes.

Two bolts higher, I took a fall. It was a clean fall, and everything felt fine. I started to climb back up the dihedral and grabbed a hold that looked very solid but turned out to be part of a loose boulder that was the size of a small car. It immediately went flying down the wall. I didn't weight it, kick it, or even tug on it. It was so loose that it probably would have fallen in the next rainfall. I yelled "ROCK, ROCK, ROCK!" as loud as I ever had and watched in horror as this death block approached my best friends. Luckily, the rock bounced off the wall and crashed into the 3rd-class terrain about a foot behind my friends. I started to panic, hyperventilating and tearing up. I had been certain my friends were going to die.

We all were yelling back and forth, and in between some of my deep breaths I heard, "We're OK" and "Go in direct!" I was trying to calm myself down, but all I wanted was to *not* be on the rock. I start to downclimb to the previous bolt, and when I was level with it, I loosely grabbed the quickdraw, swung out, and yelled for a "take," assuming I was on belay. In my panic, I never thought about the possibility of the boulder cutting the ropes, a tragic error. I started to plummet.

I was yelling for my life. I knew I was dead. I fell for a little while, struck a ledge, and continued to fall until I smashed into a small tree and some cactus on the 3rd-class ledges a few feet from my friends, having fallen or slid 35 to 40 meters. I was conscious for every bit of the fall, even the landing. I didn't know what to think. I was glad I survived the fall, but assumed I wasn't feeling anything because I was in shock, and that I was probably bleeding internally or and had terrible fractures. A few minutes passed, and I felt like I was semi-okay. So, with the help of my friends, I stood up. We began calling everyone we thought might help. I ended up being flown off by a helicopter that hovered over the ledge and lowered a line with a harness attached. My partners then rappelled the route.

I was in the hospital for four nights and walked out on my own two feet, with only two small fractures (one on the back of my skull, where my head hit the rock below my helmet, and also a rib), some abrasions, and bruises. I should be dead, but I'm not.

ANALYSIS

Looking back, I should have tried to calm down more after the rockfall and before I tried to move. I obviously wasn't thinking clearly, and if I'd slowed down I might have heard my partners say the ropes had been cut or I might have checked myself. It's hard to calm down in panic situations. (*Source: Foster Denney.*)

TABLES

TABLE I: REPORTED CLIMBING ACCIDENTS

Year	Number of Accidents Reported		Total Persons Involved		Injured		Fatalities	
	USA	CAN	USA	CAN	USA	CAN	USA	CAN
1951	15	n/a	22	n/a	11	n/a	3	n/a
1952	31	n/a	35	n/a	17	n/a	13	n/a
1953	24	n/a	27	n/a	12	n/a	12	n/a
1954	31	n/a	41	n/a	31	n/a	8	n/a
1955	34	n/a	39	n/a	28	n/a	6	n/a
1956	46	n/a	72	n/a	54	n/a	13	n/a
1957	45	n/a	53	n/a	28	n/a	18	n/a
1958	32	n/a	39	n/a	23	n/a	11	n/a
1959	42	2	56	2	31	0	19	2
1960	47	4	64	12	37	8	19	4
1961	49	9	61	14	45	10	14	4
1962	71	1	90	1	64	0	19	1
1963	68	11	79	12	47	10	19	2
1964	53	11	65	16	44	10	14	3
1965	72	0	90	0	59	0	21	0
1966	67	7	80	9	52	6	16	3
1967	74	10	110	14	63	7	33	5
1968	70	13	87	19	43	12	27	5
1969	94	11	125	17	66	9	29	2
1970	129	11	174	11	88	5	15	5
1971	110	17	138	29	76	11	31	7
1972	141	29	184	42	98	17	49	13
1973	108	6	131	6	85	4	36	2
1974	96	7	177	50	75	1	26	5
1975	78	7	158	22	66	8	19	2
1976	137	16	303	31	210	9	53	6
1977	121	30	277	49	106	21	32	11
1978	118	17	221	19	85	6	42	10
1979	100	36	137	54	83	17	40	19
1980	191	29	295	85	124	26	33	8
1981	97	43	223	119	80	39	39	6
1982	140	48	305	126	120	43	24	14
1983	187	29	442	76	169	26	37	7

Year	Number of Accidents Reported		Total Persons Involved		Injured		Fatalities	
	USA	CAN	USA	CAN	USA	CAN	USA	CAN
1984	182	26	459	63	174	15	26	6
1985	195	27	403	62	190	22	17	3
1986	203	31	406	80	182	25	37	14
1987	192	25	377	79	140	23	32	9
1988	156	18	288	44	155	18	24	4
1989	141	18	272	36	124	11	17	9
1990	136	25	245	50	125	24	24	4
1991	169	20	302	66	147	11	18	6
1992	175	17	351	45	144	11	43	6
1993	132	27	274	50	121	17	21	1
1994	158	25	335	58	131	25	27	5
1995	168	24	353	50	134	18	37	7
1996	139	28	261	59	100	16	31	6
1997	158	35	323	87	148	24	31	13
1998	138	24	281	55	138	18	20	1
1999	123	29	248	69	91	20	17	10
2000	150	23	301	36	121	23	24	7
2001	150	22	276	47	138	14	16	2
2002	139	27	295	29	105	23	34	6
2003	118	29	231	32	105	22	18	6
2004	160	35	311	30	140	16	35	14
2005	111	19	176	41	85	14	34	7
2006	109	n/a	227	n/a	89	n/a	21	n/a
2007	113	n/a	211	n/a	95	n/a	15	n/a
2008	112	n/a	203	n/a	96	n/a	19	n/a
2009	126	n/a	240	n/a	112	n/a	23	n/a
2010	185	n/a	389	n/a	151	n/a	34	n/a
2011	157	n/a	348	n/a	109	n/a	29	n/a
2012	140	15	309	36	121	12	30	2
2013	143	11	283	24	100	5	21	4
2014	112	10	170	19	89	8	28	1
2015	173	20	258	52	111	16	37	4
2016	175	23	302	58	134	17	32	6
2017	162	24	n/a	n/a	116	19	34	2
2018	187	17	n/a	n/a	198	12	17	5
TOTAL	8,005	1,078	n/a	n/a	6,679	804	1,713	316

TABLE II: REPORTED ACCIDENTS BY LOCATION

Geographic Districts	1951–2017 Number of Accidents	Deaths	2018 Number of Accidents	Deaths	Injuries
Canada*					
Alberta	579	149	11	5	8
British Columbia	350	131	3	0	2
Yukon Territory	43	28	1	0	0
New Brunswick	1	0			
Ontario	40	9	2	0	2
Québec	33	10			
East Arctic	8	2			
West Arctic	2	2			
United States					
Alaska	635	224	15	2	17
Arizona, Nevada, Texas	133	26	8	0	8
Atlantic–North	1221	163			
Atlantic–South	249	44			
California	1595	342	35	2	35
Central	144	18			
Colorado	1006	258	25	0	29
Montana, Idaho, South Dakota	103	41	1	0	1
Oregon	274	131	15	2	19
Utah, New Mex.	243	75	10	1	10
Washington	2061	349	12	4	10
Wyoming	656	161	11	3	13

TABLE III: REPORTED ACCIDENTS BY CAUSE

	1951–2017 USA	*1959–2017 CAN.	2018 USA	2018 CAN.
Terrain				
Rock	5475	594	135	11
Snow	2723	382	46	2
Ice	318	24	6	4
River	25	3		
Unknown	26	11		

	1951–2017 USA	*1959–2017 CAN.	2018 USA	2018 CAN.
Ascent or Descent				
Ascent	4358	639	90	11
Descent	1472	413	65	5
Unknown	342	18	27	
Other[1]	46	4	5	1
Immediate Cause				
Fall or slip on rock	4231	320	62	6
Fall on snow or ice	1215	223	15	2
Falling rock, ice, or object	711	153	15	1
Exceeding abilities / Inexperience	605	36	7	
Illness[2]	469	28	3	
Stranded / Lost	428	66	23	1
Avalanche	335	137	4	3
Rappel Failure / Error[3]	429	58	10	3
Lowering Error[7]	17	2	12	
Exposure	287	14	3	
Loss of control / Glissade	246	18	2	
Nut / cam pulled out	297	11	1	
Failure to follow route	259	36		
Fall into crevasse / moat	197	52		
Faulty use of crampons	127	7	1	
Piton / ice screw pulled out	95	13		
Ascending too fast	80	0	2	
Skiing[4]	81	16	4	
Lightning	68	7		
Equipment failure	18	3		
Other[5]	634	42	6	1
Unknown	86	12	17	
Contributory Causes				
Climbing unroped	1116	174	7	2
Exceeding abilities / Inexperience	1072	208	27	1
Placed no / inadequate protection	937	108	29	4
Inadequate equipment / clothing	778	77	16	1
Weather	546	77	5	5
Climbing alone	473	74	7	
No helmet	395	76	11	1
Inadequate belay[6]	310	30	7	
Nut / cam pulled out	256	33	19	3

	1951–2017 USA	*1959–2017 CAN.	2018 USA	2018 CAN.
Poor position	258	32	5	
Darkness	187	23	7	
Party separated	142	12	1	
Loose rock / failure to test holds	138	51	7	2
Piton / ice screw pulled out	87	15	1	
Failed to follow directions / route	114	19	22	1
Exposure	68	16		
Illness[2]	43	9	6	1
Equipment failure	23	7	3	
Other[5]	326	103	9	1
Age of Individuals				
Under 15	1249	12	3	
15-20	1359	204	7	
21-25	1637	262	32	
26-30	1570	215	19	3
31-35	2180	18	24	1
36-50	3571	146	26	1
Over 50	454	37	15	
Unknown	2348	609	89	13
Sex[7]				
Male	383	52	140	11
Female	118	12	25	1
Not known	75	12	51	6
Experience Level				
None/Little	1950	308	38	1
Moderate (1 to 3 years)	1832	362	38	3
Experienced	2575	502	47	9
Unknown	2766	617	97	5
Month				
January	280	28	3	
February	260	62	7	
March	405	75	6	4
April	502	44	12	1
May	1058	70	28	
June	1317	81	32	3
July	2150	273	20	2

	1951–2017 USA	*1959–2017 CAN.	2018 USA	2018 CAN.
August	1231	208	12	3
September	2094	82	9	2
October	541	44	15	
November	261	24	8	1
December	139	27	5	1
Unknown	55	3	30	
Type of Injury/Illness (Data since 1984)				
Fracture	1763	255	78	5
Laceration	881	84	21	2
Abrasion	438	80	19	
Bruise	609	89	20	1
Sprain / strain	498	38	7	
Head injury/traumatic brain injury	370	34	29	2
Hypothermia	185	19	2	1
Frostbite	161	13	2	
Dislocation	182	16	3	
Puncture	58	14	6	
Acute mountain sickness	54	0	1	
HAPE	94	1	3	
HACE	38	1	2	
Other[8]	465	62	23	2
None	404	205	29	2

N.B. Data change: The 1986 and 1997 editions had some repeat data from previous years. The corrections are reflected in the cumulative data.

[1] Some accidents happen when climbers are at the top or bottom of a route. They may be belaying or setting up a rappel, for example. This category was created in 2001. The category "unknown" is primarily because of solo climbers.

[2] These are illnesses/injuries that led directly or indirectly to an accident, such as HAPE.

[3] These included anchor failure, uneven ropes, no knots in rope ends, pendulum swings, and attaching device incorrectly. Prior years' data included some lowering errors.

[4] This category covers ski mountaineering. Backcountry ski touring or snowshoeing incidents, including those involving avalanches, are not counted in these tables.

[5] These included failure to self-arrest, anchor failure, knee stuck in crack, speed climbing, using hardware store rope or carabiners, snakebite, skiing fall caused by sled, and impact by falling tree.

[6] These included miscommunication and ineffective belay.

[7] Categories introduced in 2016. The lowering errors included rope too short, miscommunication, and no knot in rope end.

[8] These included rope burns, carbon monoxide poisoning, partial amputation, collapsed lung, and other injuries.

Note: Injuries are counted only once in each category for a given incident. For example, an accident that results in three broken bones will only be listed once under "Fracture."

MOUNTAIN
RESCUE
ASSOCIATION

+ Saving lives through rescue and mountain safety education
+ Accrediting rescue teams in mountain rescue disciplines
+ 100 rescue teams / 2,000 professional volunteer mountain rescuers
+ MRA teams perform 5,000 search & rescue operations in the U.S. each year
+ Member teams do not charge for their services

Go to www.mra.org to learn more and find backcountry safety information.

Photo: © Dale Atkins

Courage. Commitment. Compassion.
www.mra.org